# JESUS OF THE GOSPELS

# JESUS OF THE GOSPELS

## TEACHER, STORYTELLER, FRIEND, MESSIAH

## Arthur E. Zannoni

## ST. ANTHONY MESSENGER PRESS
Cincinnati, Ohio

*Nihil Obstat:* Rev. Thomas Richstatter, O.F.M., S.T.D.
Rev. Robert L. Hagedorn

*Imprimi Potest:* Rev. John Bok, O.F.M., Provincial

*Imprimatur:* Most Reverend Carl K. Moeddel, V.G.
Archdiocese of Cincinnati
June 12, 1996

The *nihil obstat* and *imprimatur* are a declaration that a book is considered to be free from doctrinal or moral error. It is not implied that those who have granted the *nihil obstat* and *imprimatur* agree with the contents, opinions or statements expressed.

Sections of Chapters Two and Three were originally published in the December 1993 and 1994 issues of *Catholic Update* and the October 1995 issue of *Scripture From Scratch,* published by St. Anthony Messenger Press.

Cover and book design by Mary Alfieri
Electronic format and pagination by Sandra Digman

Cover painting "Blessed Are They Who Have Not Seen and Yet Have Believed," copyright ©1977 by Jack Pullen.

ISBN 0-86716-241-4

Published by St. Anthony Messenger Press

Printed in the U.S.A.

# Contents

## ACKNOWLEDGMENTS

No book is ever the product of just one individual. In many ways this book is the result of my many years of teaching, so I begin by thanking all of the students who have required me to wrestle honestly with Jesus over the years.

Individually, I want to thank Betty Bigelbach, retired reference librarian at John Ireland Library, for her invaluable research assistance; all the staff at St. Anthony Messenger Press: Lisa Biedenbach, Father Jack Wintz, Diane Houdek, John Bookser Feister and especially Carol Luebering, for their constant encouragement; Leslie Carney for her listening ear and her expertise and enterprise in typing the entire manuscript and innumerable hours of word processing and reediting; my dear friend and fellow writer, Bill Huebsch, who is a constant support; David Haas, who spurred me to a speedy completion of the manuscript; Sue Martin for invaluable suggestions; and Michael Shermis, friend and dynamic editor.

Finally, I must express my greatest appreciation to my spouse, Kathleen Flannery Zannoni, for her love, care, encouragement, affirmation, trust and support throughout the tedious process called writing. Without her constant presence this book would never have been completed.

# Introduction

We all love adventures—not only the kind that are displayed on movie and television screens, but the smaller adventures of life: enjoying a sunset, listening to a favorite piece of music, being with a special person, going on vacation.

The story of Jesus in the Gospels is quite an adventure. It happened "once upon a time in a far-off land, long, long ago." The characters include criminals and priests, men and women, rich and poor, uneducated and educated, sick and healthy. They all seem so ordinary, yet they desire to know and relate to Jesus.

Some follow Jesus out of curiosity, others out of commitment; others journey with him as critics. In many ways, the Gospel characters are like all of us. They and we are not quite sure what to make of Jesus and are somewhat confused by an encounter with him.

The Jesus whom we discover in the Gospels is both elusive and complex. The Gospel writers cannot agree completely on whether to present him as a carpenter, a rabbi, a storyteller, a party-goer, a miracle-worker, a healer, an exorcist, a poet, a mystic, a revolutionary, the Messiah, a prophet, God's Son. The reason for this is that Jesus, like all persons, remains to some extent a mystery. He defies both definition and easy explanation.

Exploring who Jesus is, as portrayed in the Gospels, is the purpose of this book. We will wrestle with both his identity and his teachings. Like any adventure, this will be both exciting and interesting. After all, for almost two thousand years the world and the Church have been trying to respond to the question, "Who do people say Jesus is?" We will join in that centuries-old search. The name given to this enterprise is *Christology*—meaning, literally, "words" (Greek *logia*) "about the Christ" (Greek *christos*). We will discover that the roots of Christology lie in the historical Jesus, the Scriptures and the ever-developing traditions of the Church.

This book will *not* attempt to look at all of that. Instead, it will provide the view of Jesus found in the Gospels placed in the context of the Jewish and Greco-Roman world of the first century of the Common Era.[1] It will make no attempt to look at the writings of Saint Paul or other New Testament books. While these writings and other Christian Scriptures do offer differing views of Jesus than those found in the Gospels, they are beyond our scope here.

It may be helpful, while reading the book, to make a distinction between the Jesus of history and the Christ of faith. "Jesus of history" refers to a historical person, Jesus of Nazareth, and the various facts about his life: what he said and did and how he affected the lives of those who lived with him and knew him. The "Christ of faith" refers to what people *believe* about Jesus of Nazareth (for example, that he is the Son of God).

In the four Gospels, we encounter the Christ of faith, for the authors of the Gospels were primarily concerned with proclaiming what they *believed* about Jesus. The Gospels also give us information about the Jesus of history. In this book, we will attempt to look at both.

To enhance the reader's understanding, I have provided discussion questions at the end of each chapter. For those who may wish to delve further, I also offer a list of books for personal reading. And I suggest that you keep a Bible at hand as you read so that you can look up the passages referred to in the book.

The introductory chapters explore the world into which Jesus was born (Chapter One) and his Jewishness (Chapter Two). The middle chapters reflect on who people thought Jesus was (Chapter Three), look at his preaching about the Reign of God (Chapter Four), examine Jesus as storyteller with an emphasis on his parables (Chapter Five), and ponder the stories of the meals Jesus ate and the people included in his table fellowship (Chapter Six). The final chapters explore the meaning of Jesus' death and resurrection (Chapters Seven and Eight), and conclude with a challenge to all readers about discipleship, the call to follow Jesus (Chapter Nine).

I hope this book helps everyone who seeks to know who Jesus is and who tries to live a life patterned on his. May reading it be an adventure filled with intrigue, insight and inspiration.

*Soli Deo Gloria.*

---

[1] Before the development of ecumenical and interreligious dialogue, Christians dated everything B.C. ("Before Christ") or A.D. (*Anno Domini*, "in the year of our Lord"). Our newly acquired sensitivity fosters the use of B.C.E. ("Before the Common Era") instead of B.C. and C.E. ("Common Era") instead of A.D. The term *Common Era* refers to the era Jews and Christians share in common.

CHAPTER ONE

# The World Into Which Jesus Was Born

Twenty centuries ago, born in poverty and raised in an
obscure Galilean village in Palestine, a small country no
bigger than New Jersey, there emerged on the stage of world
history Jesus of Nazareth. This itinerant Galilean preacher has
affected the world like no other person.

He was not fully appreciated until after his brutal death,
which is not unusual. We often seem to appreciate wonderful
people only after they are gone.

Nearly two millennia have passed since the days when
Jesus walked the dusty roads of Palestine, and we are still
asking, "Who is this man?" People called him many names
during his earthly life—Son of Man, rabbi, the Nazarene,
servant, a prophet—and still we ask. We need constantly to
seek answers to that question, primarily because of what
people believed about him after his death and resurrection.
The titles Jesus then received come so easily to us now that
we lose touch with what they originally meant. We often fail
to realize the magnitude these titles had for those who first
spoke them: Lord, Redeemer, Savior, Son of God, the Messiah
of God. So many people throughout history have fallen to
their knees with the overwhelming realization, "My God—
he's God!" Yet how many today find those titles nearly
meaningless? How many "put on" their faith in him with the
same sense of routine as putting on a well-worn shirt?

How do we learn about Jesus? Where can we find
information about Jesus upon which to make mature
decisions about him? There is, it seems, one major source—

1

the Gospels, all of which were composed after Jesus died.

While the Gospels are our chief sources of information about Jesus, we should note that they are not our only sources. This point needs to be considered because we will see in a moment that the people who wrote the Gospels already believed in Jesus and in the message he proclaimed about God. The Gospels are, therefore, personal accounts or faith testimonies rather than the objective kind of reporting we might expect, say, of a newspaper or television report. How can we be sure that these people who composed the Gospels didn't just make it all up out of their own imaginations? How can we be sure that Jesus actually existed?

## The Historical Evidence

Several extrabiblical and non-Christian references to Jesus show that he did exist as a historical person. A Jewish historian, Flavius Josephus (c. 37-100 C.E.), mentions Jesus in his book *Antiquities of the Jews*, which he composed around the years 93 to 94 C.E., roughly sixty years after Jesus' death. As a Jew and later a member of the Roman Imperial Court, Josephus had no reason to accept the historical reality of Jesus without some sound basis. Josephus discusses disturbances caused by the Jews when Pontius Pilate was Procurator of Judea (26-36 C.E.). In his reflections, he mentions Jesus and calls him "a wise man."

Roman authors make several references to Jesus as well. Suetonius (c. 69 C.E.), a Roman historian and lawyer, compiled biographies of several Roman emperors around the year 120 C.E. He says that Claudius expelled the Jews from Rome because of the riots in which they were constantly involved at the instigation of the *Christos*. Though there is some debate on this, scholars generally agree that "the *Christos*" refers to "the Christ," a title applied to Jesus by his followers.

Another Roman historian, Tacitus (c. 55-117 C.E.), also refers to Jesus in his writings. He writes in his *Annals* of a fire that burned Rome in 64 C.E., for which the Emperor Nero blamed the Christians. Though Tacitus was apparently skeptical about Nero's claim, Tacitus appeared to have had no great love for the strange group of people called Christians. He refers to them as receiving their name from Christ, who was executed by a sentence from the procurator Pontius Pilate in the reign of Tiberius.

Pliny the Younger (c. 62-113 C.E.) was governor of a Roman province of Bithynia in Asia Minor. About the year 110, he wrote to the emperor Trajan for advice on what to do about the Christians. The Roman state was always concerned about the growth of any political or religious sect, and the Christian community baffled them. Though Pliny mentions Jesus, he offers no new information about him.

Lucien of Samosota (c. 120-180 C.E.), a traveling lecturer and sophist, speaks of Jesus as the "first lawgiver" of the Christians, who persuaded them that they are all brothers and sisters of one another. Lucien refers to them as "worshiping that crucified sophist himself [Jesus] and living under his laws."

The point in mentioning these nonbiblical, non-Christian sources is not to claim that they offer to us more information about Jesus than we can find in the Gospels. On the contrary, without the Gospels we would have only vague and confusing references to Jesus in historical records. Without the Gospels, Jesus would be little more than a rumor from the past. But these sources do demonstrate that their authors simply presumed the historical existence of Jesus and found the movement based on his life and teachings—later called Christianity—worthy of at least a brief mention in their writings.

Still, one overwhelming fact remains: If we want to know about Jesus to any degree, we must turn to the Christian Scriptures, and specifically to the Gospels.[1]

## The Christian Scriptures—Testimonies of Faith

The twenty-seven books that make up the Christian Scriptures contain a variety of materials representing not only different authors, but also different styles or types of writing. There are personal letters, homilies or sermons from early liturgical or worship services, some highly symbolic and imaginative writings and, of course, the four Gospels. The different authors of the Gospels wrote their testimonials at different times and places to different audiences. While the Gospels are probably the best known section of the Christian Scriptures, they comprise only a small portion of the religious literature to which the Church looks to encounter Jesus, his person, his teachings and his promises.

The Gospels are not biographies in the same sense that we would view that kind of writing today. It is fair to say we will completely misunderstand the purpose and meaning of the Gospels if we view them as video recordings of the life and work of Jesus. They simply do not offer us that kind of detailed information. We can't give a precise date for Jesus' birth or provide anything like a complete description of his parents or his disciples. We have no idea how tall or short Jesus was, whether he was handsome or unattractive or whether he was formally educated. In short, we lack a great deal of the kind of information a biographer would normally provide in an accurate portrayal of a person.

If, then, the Gospels are not biographies of Jesus, what are they? A clue can be found in the very word *gospel* itself. We derive this word from the Middle English word *Godspell*, which means "good news" or "glad tidings." That word, in turn, was a translation of the Greek word *evangelion*, also meaning the proclamation or announcement of good news. So the first verse in Mark's Gospel identifies clearly what the Gospel is about: "The beginning of the Good News of Jesus Christ, the Son of God" (Mark 1:1).

We learn from the very word *gospel* that the purpose of these writings is to announce a message of faith in Jesus. They are, in other words, *testimonies of faith* written by people who are totally convinced that Jesus was and is the Messiah. Note also that we call the authors of the Gospels "evangelists," based on the Greek word *evangelion*; they are, literally, "proclaimers of the Good News."

In brief, then, people of faith wrote the Gospels for people of faith about what it means to have faith in Jesus and in the God who sent him. They are neither firsthand reports nor biographies. Instead, they are post-resurrection presentations of what the early Church believed about Jesus.

The most effective way to understand the nature and purpose of the Gospels, however, is to describe how and why they were written. Scholars who have studied the Gospels have identified at least three major steps or stages in their development:

1) the actual life and works of Jesus of Nazareth and their effects on his disciples;

2) the experience of other disciples and the early Church after the death and resurrection of Jesus;

3) the actual writing of the Gospels by the evangelists, who likely served as editors or collectors or compilers of material that had gradually developed through the years.

The Church recognizes these stages of Gospel development both in the *Dogmatic Constitution on Divine Revelation* of the Second Vatican Council and in the 1965 statement of the Pontifical Biblical Commission on which the Council document was largely based.

## Stage One: Jesus of Nazareth and His Disciples

The Gospels are based upon the words and works of Jesus of Nazareth, a historical figure from Palestine some twenty centuries ago. Recognizing and accepting this claim are central to understanding and appreciating the Gospels. For if we do not base them upon events that really happened, then they teach us little more than flights of fancy or idealistic visions that we have no reason to accept, much less live our lives by.

The purpose of the Gospels is not to record events minute by minute. Instead, their intent is to convey the meaning of those events for the persons of that time and, through them, for us as well. Nevertheless, it is essential that we recognize that the foundation for the events in the Gospels is Jesus of Nazareth, a man, a historical person. When we talk about Jesus, we are definitely talking about the "Jesus of history."

What can we say about this Jesus of history that can be accepted even by those who do not accept him as the Son of God, the Messiah, the Christ? From the Gospels and other sources, we know that he was born a Jew in Bethlehem of Judea during the reign of King Herod (see Matthew 2:1). While growing up in Nazareth in the northern province of Galilee, he apparently learned and practiced the trade of carpentry.

Around age thirty he began a public career of preaching and teaching, proclaiming the beginning of a new era (the Reign of God, as he called it). Some people saw him as a wonder-worker. His preaching and action stirred great interest among the Jewish people, leading some to proclaim him as a great prophet and others to reject him as a sorcerer, a magician, a blasphemer and a threat to the Roman state. Those in power eventually brought him to trial, found him guilty of crimes under Roman law, and had him executed by crucifixion.

This much people of any religious persuasion or belief could accept simply by being open to the available historical records. But those who followed this Jesus and others who would eventually write about him in the Gospels clearly believed him to be much more than just a Jewish man, more than just Jesus of Nazareth, the itinerant preacher, more than simply the Jesus of history. They believed him to be the Risen One who conquered death and ushered in the Reign of God.

The followers of Jesus claimed that he did not remain dead. Instead, they experienced him alive again and present among them some three days after the Roman authorities savagely executed him on a cross. This became the identifying mark of all those who claimed Jesus as their Lord and Savior: belief in his Resurrection. So central to the lives of Christians is the conviction of Jesus' living presence after death that Paul was to say that "if Christ has not been raised, then our proclamation has been in vain and your faith has been in vain" (1 Corinthians 15:14).

We will discuss the Resurrection in more detail in Chapter Eight. The point here is that the first stage in the development of the Gospels was Jesus' disciples' experience not only of his earthly existence, his message and his actions, but especially of his rising from the dead. This event made all that he said and did before that acceptable as truth. Without the Resurrection, the followers of Jesus would likely have dispersed in fear of their own execution. But with the experience of the risen Jesus, they boldly went forth from their places of hiding and began proclaiming the Good News ...that God has made him both Lord and Messiah, this Jesus whom you crucified" (Acts 2:36b).

Some immediately rejected that proclamation as foolhardy, ridiculous, insane. For them, the Jesus of history would always remain a carpenter's son who preached a radical message and paid for it with his life. But others, convinced that Jesus was raised by God from death itself, believed he truly was and is forever Lord and Savior. For these people, the Jesus of history was clearly much more: the Christ of faith.

## Stage Two: The Disciples and the Early Church

Imagine yourself in the position of Jesus' early disciples. You walk with Jesus. You listen to his inspiring message proclaimed in synagogues and on hillsides. You touch him and are touched by him. You witness the marvelous impact he makes on everyone he meets. Gradually, you find yourself enthralled with this fellow. He speaks to all your hopes and dreams, and you are certain that in this man from Nazareth you have discovered fullness of life.

Then you witness the horror of his crucifixion. You see the man you love so deeply stretched out against the sky, nailed to a beam of wood, carrying all your dreams and hopes along with him to his death. You and your friends who had also believed in him run away in fear. You are shattered. You feel hopeless. You are convinced that all he promised was a sham, a lie—at the very least a terrible mistake.

But then comes Easter Sunday. Suddenly, you have an overwhelming experience of him as present again. He is alive, truly with you. He is risen! This man has even conquered death! Incredible joy and peace surge into your heart and you run from your place of hiding, shouting the Good News from the rooftops, "He's alive. Everything he told us is true!"

What would you do next? You would tell others—exactly as the early Christians did. Instead of writing about their experiences with Jesus, they began an intense missionary campaign to proclaim orally to all people the meaning of the birth, life, ministry, passion, death and resurrection of Jesus. In a matter of decades, the proclamation of this Good News of Jesus spread like wildfire throughout the Roman Empire.

The process of picking and choosing what to remember about Jesus was initiated within the context of this preaching of the Good News throughout the empire. The early Christians used incidents from Jesus' life and teaching to instruct people who were interested in joining the community of faith. Reflections on his life in terms of the Hebrew Scriptures became part of this instruction. The early Christians not only recalled the words of Jesus, but also applied these words to their lived experience as they began to celebrate and live out his message in their daily lives.

In other words, nobody recorded Jesus' life and words and works in a logical, day-by-day, biographical fashion. In addition, nobody preserved all of the available information about Jesus. But the early Christians did record those events and words and teachings that had a particularly profound impact on their lives.

### Stage Three: The Early Church and the Evangelists

Jesus died around the year 30 C.E. Proclaiming the Good News about his death and resurrection and selecting recollections of his words and actions for use in preaching and worship continued for at least forty years before the early

Christians wrote the first Gospel. At this point, the editors we call evangelists decided that the kind of free-floating stories being passed on by word of mouth should be collected into organized and permanent records.

Scholars generally believe that the first Gospel written was Mark's (about the year 70 C.E., some forty years after the death of Jesus). They suggest Matthew and Luke perhaps wrote their Gospels during the early 80's, and John not until as late as 90 to 95 C.E. We will say more about these editors and their unique Gospels in a moment. But first, let us address a more basic question: Why were the Gospels developed at all?

There are at least two answers.

By the latter half of the first century, it was apparent that the Church would probably be around for a long time. The early expectations of an immediate return by Jesus and the certain end of the world gradually faded with the passing years. With the realization that the original eyewitnesses of Jesus were dying off and that the Church did have a future, it became necessary to find a way to preserve its teachings and pass them on to future generations. This was one motive for developing the Gospels.

The second was also a continued need to instruct and inspire the communities of faith already formed throughout the empire. Each of the Gospel writers gathered all the traditions about Jesus into a story in response to the needs of a particular audience in a particular location at a particular time. Thus, each Gospel is unique. Certain incidents recorded by one Gospel writer are described or expressed differently by another. No one Gospel, therefore, provides a completely accurate understanding of Jesus. Gospels are intentionally interpretive; they are not videotaped biographies of Jesus. They are historically and culturally conditioned *testimonies of faith*.

## The Four Faith Testimonies

The Gospels, then, are not simply the result of four individuals sitting down independently to write life histories of Jesus based on their personal recollections. Each evangelist had a wealth of available material, a particular audience in mind and a particular theology to present.

### Mark's Gospel

*Mark* was a common name during the time of Jesus; the Mark credited with writing the first Gospel could literally have been just about anyone. None of the Gospels names its author directly. All the Gospel authors are anonymous. The names we attach to each Gospel represent the opinions of the early Church about the authors. The author of Mark is, at times, associated with a certain John Mark mentioned in Acts 12:12. A group of Christians regularly met at his mother's house for prayer. Some believed this John Mark to be the author of this Gospel. This supposition, however, would be hard to prove.

For whom was this Gospel written? Scholars traditionally accept that Mark wrote his Gospel in Rome for the Church there, and that it was intended for non-Jewish readers, Gentiles. Customs that Jews would have readily understood, for instance, are explained in Mark's Gospel in a way that suggests the audience is not familiar with them.

Mark wrote his Gospel sometime between 65 and 70 C.E., that is, 35 to 40 years after the death of the historical Jesus. There is a heavy sense of suffering in Mark, with many references to trials and persecutions. Some scholars suggest this reflects the persecution of the Christians by the Roman emperor Nero who, as we mentioned earlier, blamed the Christians for the burning of Rome in the year 64 C.E. For our purposes, we will settle on the year 70 as roughly the date of writing.

Why was this Gospel written? Mark's Gospel stresses the human suffering of Jesus and his passion and death, perhaps as a way to relate to the Christians, who were suffering terrible persecution at the time. The central point of his entire Gospel is to describe the death of Jesus; and everything else is by way of introduction. It seems certain, then, that one of Mark's intentions was to explain to the members of the early Church that suffering is an essential part of Christian life and to give them the courage to endure it as Jesus had. There is also a stress on Jesus' humanity in Mark's Gospel, where we see Jesus expressing strong emotions. Mark was trying to counter the claim some made during his day that Jesus was not truly human, but a divine being who simply pretended to be a man. Mark's account makes it clear that Jesus was truly human—one who embraced human suffering.

### Luke's Gospel

The Gospel of Luke is the first volume of a two-volume work. (The second is the Acts of the Apostles.) A persistent tradition holds that the author was a physician, a well-educated Gentile convert to Christianity. Paul identified a person named Luke as a doctor, and some scholars have pointed out that parts of the Gospel of Luke suggest some medical knowledge. This point is probably an exaggeration, given the limited evidence.

Luke is mentioned in the Christian Scriptures as a companion of Paul (see Colossians 4:14; 2 Timothy 4:11). At one point, Paul says that Luke was not a Jew. If this is true, then the author of Luke and Acts is probably the only non-Jewish writer of the Christian Scriptures. In actuality, the author of the Gospel of Luke is anonymous.

When was the Gospel of Luke written? It is quite difficult to date. It appears that the author had Mark's Gospel available when he was writing, since he uses some material directly from that Gospel. Luke probably was composed sometime in the 80's.

Why was the Gospel of Luke written? At the very beginning of his Gospel, Luke tells a certain Theophilus, to whom he is addressing his Gospel, that he is writing "so that you may know the truth concerning the things about which you have been instructed" (Luke 1:4). Luke claims that he has studied all of the available accounts and wants to offer his own "orderly account." He sets out early to show the continuity of Christianity with the Judaism of the Hebrew Scriptures. Throughout his Gospel, Luke emphasizes the central role of the Holy Spirit in Jesus' life. He closes his Gospel by stressing the continuing presence of Jesus through his Spirit after his death and resurrection. Perhaps he was trying to support those readers who were discouraged that Jesus had not yet returned.

Another major feature of Luke's Gospel is that it emphasizes the Christian message is for everyone—Jews and Gentiles, men and women, rich and poor. There is a continuing reminder of the joy shared by those who experience God's forgiving love in Jesus. The Gospel of Luke, therefore, clearly depicts a Jesus who deeply loves all people.

## Matthew's Gospel

There is no clear agreement on the author or the date of Matthew's Gospel. Early in the history of the Church, tradition had it that the author was a disciple of Jesus and, therefore, an eyewitness to his life and work. The author, however, seems to have used almost all of Mark's Gospel, and has much in common with Luke's account as well. It would be strange that an eyewitness of these events would rely so heavily upon other sources.

Regarding the date of writing, most scholars opt for a date between 80 and 100 C.E. In the long view, these questions are less essential to us than the fact that Matthew's Gospel contains so much of Mark and Luke and is so thorough and well organized that it quickly became the most popular and widely used Gospel in the early Church.

A close reading of Matthew's Gospel will enable you to see that it is very different in structure from Mark and Luke. The pattern of this Gospel copies that of the first five books of the Hebrew Scriptures, showing a desire by the author to show the Jews in particular that Jesus was clearly the Messiah they had awaited. It places special emphasis on demonstrating that all of Jesus' life was a fulfillment of the promises made by

God to Israel by quoting extensively from the Hebrew
Scriptures, often from the books of the prophets.

Jesus, for example, is presented as a true teacher of the
Jewish law. Matthew also shows interest in the Church itself,
which may provide a clue to his intent. The Gospel contains
Jesus' teaching in a clear and thorough way so that it can
serve well in instructing new converts to the faith. Matthew's
sensitivity to the continuity between Christianity and Judaism
also made the Gospel valuable to Jews who were asking
about the faith.

### John's Gospel

The Fourth Gospel—the Gospel of John—is quite different
from the other three. Matthew, Mark, and Luke are similar in
so many respects that the popular term for them is "Synoptic
Gospels." The word *synoptic* suggests that they can be best
understood when seen or looked at together or side by side.
John's Gospel, on the other hand, is unique; a fact that you
can experience, if not fully understand, with just a quick
reading of a few sections.

There is wide disagreement over the author of the fourth
Gospel and we may never resolve the question. Church
tradition for years suggested that John the Apostle wrote the
Gospel at the end of a very long life after much prayer,
reflection and personal experience of actually living out his
faith in Jesus. This would account for its reflective, prayerful
and thoughtful style. But many scholars feel that the Gospel
was not written until the year 90 C.E. at the earliest. Thus, it
would be highly unlikely, if not impossible, for a disciple of
Jesus to have written it. Mark 10:39 hints that John the
Apostle was martyred, while it appears from John 21:23 that
the author of this Gospel was not. It may be best to refer to
this Gospel as being composed by "the community of the
Beloved Disciple."

The late date of the Gospel of John helps us to gain an
understanding of its unique style and multiple purposes.
Many years had passed since Jesus of Nazareth walked
among the people of Palestine, years during which there was

a continually deepening understanding of who he truly was.

Only after the Resurrection did the early Christians fully recognize Jesus as the Christ, the Messiah and, even later, as the Son of God. The more time people had to reflect on these realities and their implications, the more central to their teaching and preaching they became. In John's Gospel, we see a much stronger attempt to present a profound and prayerful understanding of Jesus as the divine Son of God than we find in the Synoptic Gospels.

Many scholars therefore feel that if we are to attempt an accurate historical portrait of Jesus as he lived and taught in Palestine, we should rely more heavily on the Synoptic Gospels than on John. This does not mean that John's Gospel is not truthful. The truths it attempts to share are, however, more deeply theological and reflective than those in the other Gospels.

On the other hand, the almost poetically prayerful nature of John's Gospel and its familiar and treasured imagery of Jesus as the Light of the World, the Bread of Life and the Good Shepherd have made this Gospel a favored source for meditation on the divine significance of Jesus' life.

In sum, these Gospels were not formulated in a vacuum. The writers composed them over a period of time in a particular geographical place and culture. All these factors greatly influenced their composition. We will now look briefly at that world in order to enhance our understanding.

## The World of Jesus and His Daily Life

To enter the world at the time of Jesus, we need to start with the land in which he lived. This land—the modern state of Israel—stretched just about 145 miles from north to south, and between 25 to 87 miles from its western coast at the Mediterranean Sea to its eastern borders. The Scriptures refer to the land in a variety of ways: "the land of Israel," the "land of Canaan," "the Promised Land" or the "land of Judah." The Greeks named it after the Philistines who had inhabited the coastal area at one time: Palestine. This small region (a car can travel from one corner to another in just a few hours) is the only world that Jesus ever knew.

Israel's small size may also explain in part the profound love the people had for their land; they knew it personally. In Jesus' day, people usually walked from town to town. Jesus' contemporaries were great walkers, thinking nothing of walking great distances. A good walker could go from Nazareth to Jerusalem in about two days. The Gospels show continual movement from one place to another.

Within this confined area, however, there is tremendous geographical diversity. The Gospels speak of lake shores and hillsides, of deserts and forests. In the south, the area surrounding the Dead Sea is desolate and forbidding, while the land around the Sea of Galilee to the north is lush and inviting. Rainfall and temperatures vary greatly between the north and the south

Such variation in the climate gave rise to a variety of vegetation and foliage in the land that Jesus knew. Trees such as juniper and oak were common. Olive and fig trees were prized for the fruit and oil they provided. People made their wine from the wonderful grapes. Common grains included wheat, oats and barley. Bread was the essential food of Jesus' day. To "break bread" meant to have a full meal, just as it does today when we speak of "breaking bread together." The people of those days treated bread with great respect and enacted laws governing its use. They ate yeast bread regularly and unleavened bread during the Passover festival.

In Jesus' day, people ate very little meat, which was primarily a luxury for the wealthy. The most common food, other than bread, was fish; together these formed the daily meal. Fish was dried or salted to preserve it; fresh, it was cooked over a charcoal fire, as we read about Jesus doing during a Resurrection appearance (see John 21:9). Fruit and nuts were readily available.

People often were flexible about the times they ate their meals. At formal meals, they ate with their hands and in a reclining, rather than sitting, position.

Most homes were simple, neither large nor impressive.

Most people were part of what we would call today the lower class. Their homes were usually one-room cubes made of clay, which they sometimes baked into bricks. The room was frequently divided in two, with people living on one side and animals on the other. Sometimes they built their houses into the side of a hill so that part of the house was a cave.

People worked at a variety of occupations in Jesus' day. Many were farmers and shepherds, and images from these occupations fill the Gospels. Fishing was another common and respected occupation, as were trades—the Bible mentions about twenty-five of them, ranging from the carpentry of Jesus and Joseph to the tent-making of Saint Paul.

## The Political World of Jesus

As a Jew, Jesus was a minority person in the Greco-Roman world; as a Galilean, he was a minority person within official Judaism, which centered in Jerusalem. Many urban Jews of his day might have asked, "Can anything good come out of Galilee?" (see John 7:52). The region of Galilee was known for both political revolution and Jewish reform movements.

Trying to make sense out of this world of Jesus' day is not always easy for the modern reader. A short history lesson will be helpful.

In brief, the Greeks dominated ancient Palestine from 323 to 142 B.C.E. The greatest Greek, of course, was Alexander the Great. He lived a short life of thirty-three years (356-323 B.C.E.); in that time, however, he conquered much of the Mediterranean world and lands as far east as India.

After his death, the leading generals of his army divided the land Alexander had conquered. Two of the generals, Seleucid and Ptolemy, and their successors, would dominate ancient Palestine for one hundred fifty years. The city of Antioch in Syria, just north of Israel was the base of the Seleucid dynasty; Alexandria in Egypt, to the southwest of ancient Palestine, was the base of the Ptolemean dynasty.

For about the first one hundred years of Greek domination, the Egyptian Ptolemies ruled Israel with little interference in the internal affairs of the Jews. Nevertheless, Greek culture (also known as Hellenism) had a subtle impact upon the people of ancient Palestine. Most notable was the increased use of the Greek language throughout the country. In the northern region of Israel (Galilee), where the Seleucids ruled, the Greeks profoundly influenced all levels of the culture—so much so that the Bible refers to the region as "Galilee of the Gentiles." (Gentiles are non-Jews.) By Jesus' time, a Jew born in Galilee was "born on the wrong side of the tracks."

The more tolerant Greek occupation practiced by the Ptolemies ended in the year 198 B.C.E., when all of Israel came under the control of the Seleucids. The Seleucids needed increased revenue because the Romans had inflicted a naval defeat upon them and demanded an enormous amount of money. To pay them and to support their war efforts, the Seleucids began to tax Israel heavily. Their demands shattered any peace or goodwill that had previously existed between the Greeks and Jews.

Reactions to Greek rule and influence varied along two lines. The wealthy landowners and priestly class tried to get along with the foreigners, because they had the most to lose in any conflict with them. The other side, a group called the *Hasidim* or "pious ones," resented the Seleucids and thought that any compromise or accommodation with them amounted to a rejection of their Jewish faith. This was the context for many disagreements that appear in the Gospels, especially the tension between the Sadducees and the Pharisees.

Seleucid domination eventually lead to Jewish rebellion. To extend his control over the land, the ruler of the Seleucids tried to take possession of the land held by the Ptolemeans in Egypt. The Romans stepped into the conflict, however, and stopped the Seleucids. Some rebels within the Jewish community were heartened by this and thought they could overthrow the Seleucids. They were wrong. The Seleucid ruler, Antiochus IV Epiphanes, took out his rage on the rebelling Jews. He not only crushed the rebellion, but also sacked Jerusalem, desecrated the Temple, and built an altar to the Greek god Zeus in the Holy of Holies, the most sacred part of the Temple.

Antiochus completely underestimated the power of the people and their religious convictions. All of Judea erupted in outrage at what the Seleucids had done. With the odds stacked against them, the rebelling Jews, under the leadership of a family known as the Hasmoneans, won a victory over their oppressors! The leader of the Hasmoneans, Judas Maccabeus ("the hammer") led the revolt because of his ferocious fighting ability. The story of the uprising, known as the Maccabean War or Revolt, is told in the Books of Maccabees. In the year 164 B.C.E., Judas removed the sacrilegious altar of Zeus and rededicated the sacred Temple, an event remembered and celebrated even today on the Jewish Feast of Dedication, or Hanukkah. By the year 142 B.C.E., the Seleucids had granted complete freedom to Israel; a century of national freedom followed.

During this Jewish independence, which lasted approximately from 142 to 63 B.C.E., the Hasmonean family became the political leaders. Interestingly, even before independence, a Hasmonean family member had accepted the "gift" of the high priesthood from the Seleucids. The Hasmoneans were not members of any of the accepted priestly families. By accepting the role they publicly violated the traditions of the Jewish people. This act, as interpreted by many, greatly lessened both the prestige of and respect for the priesthood, a fact witnessed in the Gospel stories.

Just as the "Hasidim" reacted to their Greek rulers earlier, so now they had to deal with their own Jewish leaders. There seems to have been no uniform reaction.

The priestly class worked out accommodations with the Hasmoneans, just as they had with the Seleucids earlier. These people became known as the Sadducees.

Some people reacted to the Hasmoneans by totally withdrawing from Jewish society to observe strict religious traditions. Scholars identify these people as the Essenes. And though they are never mentioned in the Bible, they may have influenced Jesus with their profound religious convictions and practices. Most likely the Essenes moved out of Jerusalem down to Qumran, near the Dead Sea, where the Dead Sea Scrolls were found.

Another Jewish group, the Pharisees, attempted a compromise between the political accommodation of the Sadducees and the complete withdrawal of the Essenes. An extremely important Jewish party or sect, the Pharisees, all of whom were laity, appear often in the Christian Scriptures. They categorically refused to compromise their religious beliefs and therefore lost some influence in the higher levels of religious and political power. The people highly respected the Pharisees, who gained a reputation for strict faithfulness to the covenant.

Eventually, the Hasmoneans further abused their position of power by trying to expand their base in Judea. The prejudice and bitterness between various groups in the country in Jesus' time originated during this period.

The century of independence under the Hasmonean family thus quickly deteriorated into bitter factions, nearly to the point of civil war. Finally, both the Pharisees and the Sadducees appealed to Rome for help in settling their conflicts. In 63 B.C.E., some sixty years before the birth of Jesus, the Romans occupied the country and took complete control.

When the Romans defeated a people, they carefully selected leaders from among the conquered people themselves. This procedure gave stability to the entire empire. By 37 B.C.E., the Romans had selected the Idumean Jew, Herod, to rule Israel. Herod would rule until his death in 4 B.C.E.; at the end of his reign Jesus was born. The sons of Herod would continue the dynasty until almost the end of the first century after Jesus.

As a political leader, Herod was quite successful. He combined political cunning with absolute terror. Herod was a master builder, but an incredibly cruel man. He allegedly ordered that all the prominent men of the town in which he lay dying were to be executed right at the moment of his own death so that the grief of the townspeople would be "real."

It was Herod's political ability that held the country

together during his reign. When he died, the Romans passed on his power to his three sons, Philip, Herod Antipas and Archelaus. They seem to have inherited his cruelty, but not his political savvy. Philip was the most capable. After his father's death, Philip took control of the land to the extreme northeast of ancient Palestine and there he built the town of Caesarea Philippi.

Rome gave Herod Antipas control of Galilee and Perea, a region just east of the Jordan River. This man the Gospels refer to simply as Herod, or occasionally as Herod "the tetrarch," a title based on the Greek word for *four* and referring to a person who governs one-fourth of a province. His marriage to the wife of his half-brother roused the rage of John the Baptist, leading Herod Antipas to have John beheaded (see Matthew 14:1-12). Jesus called him "that fox" in a discussion with the Pharisees (see Luke 13:31-32).

Archelaus, the third son of Herod the Great, was the worst leader of the three, but Rome gave him the most important area to rule: Judea, Samaria and Idumea. He was so inept as a leader that the Romans eventually removed him and sent him into exile. In 6 C.E., they replaced him with an official variously known as a "prefect," a "procurator" or, less often, a "governor." By the time of Jesus' public ministry, five different men had held the position. The fifth procurator began his rule in the year 26 C.E., around the beginning of Jesus' public ministry. His name was Pontius Pilate.

This confusion and division would last throughout Jesus' lifetime and beyond. Eventually, strong anti-Roman feelings led to open revolt against Rome in 67 C.E. The revolt lasted for three years. The Romans completely crushed the rebels and destroyed Jerusalem and its Temple by the year 70 C.E.

A reader of the Gospels can often become baffled by all the political intrigue. This brief history lesson may clarify some of the confusion.

### For Discussion

*1) If you were a lawyer and had to appear in a courtroom in which*

*the prosecution was going to argue against the historical*
*existence of Jesus, how would you make your case?*

2) *How has this historical presentation affected your perception and understanding of Jesus? Explain.*

3) *With which groups of Jews (Sadducees, Pharisees, Essenes, Zealots) do you think you would have been most closely aligned if you had lived in Jesus' day? Why?*

### For Further Reading

Brown, Raymond E. *Responses to 101 Questions on the Bible.* Mahwah, N.J.: Paulist Press, 1990.

Davis, Steven L. *The New Testament: A Contemporary Introduction.* San Francisco: Harper & Row, 1988.

Dicharry, Warren. *Mark, Matthew, and Luke.* Collegeville, Minn.: The Liturgical Press, 1990.

Kingsbury, J.D. *Jesus Christ in Matthew, Mark, and Luke.* Philadelphia: Fortress, 1981.

Marinelli, Anthony. *Understanding the Gospels: A Guide for Beginners.* Mahwah, N.J.: Paulist Press, 1988.

Perkins, Pheme. *Reading the New Testament,* 2nd. ed. Mahwah, N.J.: Paulist Press, 1988.

---

[1] It is becoming more common today—a time of serious interfaith dialogue—to refer to the Bible in the terms "Hebrew Scriptures" and "Christian Scriptures" rather than "Old Testament" and "New Testament." Many people feel that the use of the terms old and new is insulting to our Jewish brothers and sisters, whose sacred writings are not old to them in the sense of being outdated, outmoded or surpassed in value by later writings. There is also a tendency by Christians to lose sight of the value of the Hebrew Scriptures. After all, the term old is seldom one we use to describe things of lasting and current value. Therefore, out of respect for our Jewish friends—our ancestors in faith—and in the hope of renewing our own interest in their sacred writings, we will refer in this book to the Hebrew and Christian Scriptures rather than the Old and New Testaments.

CHAPTER TWO

# Jesus the Jew

Did you ever wonder what Jesus really looked like? What was the color of his hair? What color were his eyes? How much did he weigh? How tall was he? While these are all interesting questions, we cannot really answer them. What we do know is that Jesus was Jewish.

Jesus was not a Christian. He did not go to Mass on Sunday; he went to services on the sabbath (Saturday). He did not go to church; he worshiped at a synagogue. He did not speak Latin or English; he spoke Hebrew and Aramaic. He had a Jewish mother, which probably means he looked a lot like other Jews of his day.

His earliest followers were all Jewish. No one addressed him as "Father," "Pastor" or "Reverend." In all likelihood people addressed him as "Rabbi" ("teacher"). He did not write or read the Christian Scriptures, which others composed after his death. He did read his people's Scriptures, what Christians call the Old Testament.

Jesus never recited the rosary, chanted a litany or used a modern prayer book. He did recite the psalms; he died with one on his lips: *"Eloi, Eloi, lema sabachthani?"* "My God, my God, why have you forsaken me?" (Psalm 22:1; see Mark 15:34). He did not celebrate Christmas or Easter. He celebrated Shavuot (Feast of Weeks), Sukkot (Feast of Tabernacles) and Passover—not the Eucharist but a Seder. In all ways, Jesus was a Jew.

Jesus was a deeply faith-filled and profoundly committed Jew of his day. Unfortunately, many of us, despite our religious education and upbringing, have never understood the importance of having a solid background in Jewish religious, social and political history in order to understand Jesus. The purpose of this chapter is to explore the various factors that contribute to the Jewish roots of Jesus and our Christian faith.

## Jesus the Galilean Jew

Jesus was not an urban Jew but a rural Palestinian Jew. He lived with his family in the northern part of the country—in Galilee, a very small, rural region of ancient Palestine. This area was overwhelmingly Jewish. It was both the soil Jesus trod and the place from which his original apostles came. The part of Galilee where Jesus lived was a rich valley that stretched from the Mediterranean to the Sea of Galilee, a distance of about twenty-five miles. You can walk from Nazareth to the Sea in about three hours.

Among the important villages of this region in Jesus' day were Nazareth and Capernaum. These villages were made up of *am ha aretz*, "people of the land," the farmers and the poor who were the primary receivers of Jesus' preaching, teaching and healing. Nazareth, Jesus' hometown, was a small agricultural village in the heart of Galilee. Farmers and a few artisans made up the village's population. We know from Luke's Gospel that Nazareth had a synagogue, which Jesus attended and where he read from the Isaiah scroll (see Luke 4:16-30).

Capernaum, located north of Nazareth on the Sea of Galilee, appears to have been the center of Jesus' activity during most of his public life (see Matthew 4:12-13). It was a commercial and agricultural center with a customs house. Capernaum also had a synagogue where Jesus both healed and taught (see Luke 4:31-37).

## Jesus the Jew and Other Jews

As far as we know, in Jesus' time there were four principal Jewish sects: the Essenes, the Zealots, the Sadducees and the Pharisees.

The sect known as the Essenes, whose name may come from an Aramaic word meaning "pious," withdrew from Jerusalem and active participation in the Jerusalem Temple. They settled in the Judean wilderness in isolated monastic communities, where they studied the Scriptures and developed their rule of life. Essenes were known for such pious practices as daily prayer, prayer before and after meals, strict observance of the Sabbath, daily ritual bathing, emphasis on chastity and celibacy, the wearing of white robes as a symbol of spiritual purity, communal meals and sharing all property in common. Nowhere in the Gospels is Jesus presented as adhering to the Essene way of life.

Jesus was not a Zealot, either. Zealots were Jews (many of whom lived in Galilee) who vehemently and violently opposed the Roman occupation of Palestine. The vast majority of scholars see no evidence in any of Jesus' teachings that he opposed Roman occupation or encouraged revolt against Rome.

Jesus also was clearly set apart from the Sadducees. The Sadducees, whose name in Hebrew means "the righteous ones," were a sect in Judaism who believed in a strict interpretation of the Torah (the first five books of the Hebrew Scriptures, which Christians call the Pentateuch) and who did not believe in life after death. Jesus believed in bodily resurrection, a teaching never accepted by the Sadducees (see Mark 12:18-27).

## Jesus the Pharisee?

Contrary to common understanding, Jesus might have been close to the Pharisees, even if he did debate them vigorously. Many of Jesus' teachings and much of his style were clearly similar to those of the Pharisees. To understand this point, we need to compare the central teachings of the Pharisees to Jesus' teachings.

The Pharisees were a religious lay reform group within Judaism. At the time of Jesus, they dwelt mainly in Palestine. Their name means "separate ones" in Hebrew; it refers to their ritual observance of purity and tithing. The term *Pharisees* can also mean "the interpreters," referring to their unique interpretations of the Hebrew Scriptures.

As reformers, the Pharisees did not oppose Roman occupation, but they wanted more from the Jerusalem Temple, especially its liturgical practices and its priests. They turned their attention to strengthening the people's devotion to Torah, the heart and soul of the original covenant with God. Believing that the written Torah had become a dead letter for many, they introduced the notion that the people continually had to renew and readjust the interpretation of Torah within the framework of the changing experience of the Jewish covenantal community. The Pharisees insisted that the 613 commandments found in the written Torah remained in effect. But Jews of the Pharisees' time had carefully to rethink the commandments in light of the human needs and other realities they faced. They had to be read and lived in light of the signs of the times.

The priests attached to the Temple looked upon the precepts of the Torah more literally, and primarily in terms of sacrificial observances at the Jerusalem Temple. The priests believed these observances were the primary means of relating to God and becoming holy. The Pharisees, on the other hand, were convinced that Torah had to provide for the way human life was to be lived. In this way, the Pharisees hoped that every ordinary human action could become sacred—an act of worship. Doing "a good deed," a *mitzvah*, for another human had a status in some ways surpassing that of Temple worship. This change was truly a revolution in religious thinking.

In addition, a religious figure new in Judaism—the teacher—emerged within the Pharisaic movement. The position of teacher or rabbi differed from that of the earlier prophets and priests. The Hebrew Scriptures portrayed prophets as speaking for God, whereas priests functioned as presiders at the liturgies in the Jerusalem Temple—Zechariah, the father of John the Baptist, for example (see Luke 1:8-23). Rabbis fulfilled a twofold role in the community: they interpreted Torah and, even more important, made it concrete and relevant to the people of their day. Their principal task was instructional, not liturgical. What needs emphasizing is that a non-priestly figure, a rabbi, gradually replaced the Temple priest as the chief religious representative of Judaism's faithfulness to Torah.

Another aspect of the Pharisaic reform was the emergence of what was later called the *synagogue* (a Greek word meaning an "assembly of people"). The synagogue became a centerpiece of this reform movement, spreading throughout Palestine and the cities of the Jewish Diaspora (Jews living outside the land of Israel). Unlike the Jerusalem Temple, the synagogues were not places where priests presided and offered sacrifices. They were places where Jews studied Torah, rabbis or sages offered their interpretations and people offered prayers. They became not only "houses of God" but, far more, the "houses of the people of God."

A further characteristic of this movement was its emphasis on table fellowship as a way of strengthening relationships within the community. The Pharisees intended to extend to all the people the duties previously prescribed only for the Temple priests. In the eyes of the Pharisees, the Temple altar in Jerusalem could be replicated at every table in the household of Israel. A quiet, far-reaching reform was at hand. There was no longer any basis for assigning the priestly class a unique level of authority.

The Pharisees saw God not only as creator, giver of the covenant, an all-consuming presence, but in a special way as the *Father* or parent of each individual. Because of this universal divine parenthood, they believed that everyone had the right to address God in a direct and personal way, not just through the Temple sacrifices offered by the priests.

## Jesus and the Pharisees

Considering these similarities, there is little doubt that Jesus and the Pharisees shared many central convictions. It is to these that we now turn.

27

The first common point between Jesus and the Pharisees was their basic relationship to God. The Pharisees elevated the notion of God as *Father* (parent) to a central place in their theological outlook. So did Jesus. Story after story in the Gospels has Jesus addressing God with this title, and Jesus' central prayer begins by invoking God as "Our Father" (see Matthew 6:9-13). The general effect of this stress on divine parenthood was the same for Jesus as for the Pharisees: an enhanced appreciation of the dignity of every person and ultimately to the notion of resurrection—perpetual union with God. God revealed the fullness of this union in Jesus' bodily Resurrection.

Jesus' own public stance in the community also closely paralleled the evolving role of the Pharisaic teacher. Many times the Gospel writers call Jesus "teacher." They also present him teaching in synagogues (see, for example, Matthew 4:23; 9:35; Luke 4:15-18; John 18:20).

Jesus shared with the Pharisees a general reluctance to antagonize the Roman authorities occupying Palestine. When the disciples of the Pharisees ask him about the lawfulness of paying taxes to Caesar, Jesus responds: "Give therefore to the emperor the things that are the emperor's, and to God the things that are God's" (Matthew 22:21).

Besides the new role of the teacher (rabbi) and the synagogue, Jesus clearly picked up on another central feature of Pharisaism, Oral Torah. Oral Torah is the interpretations given by the Pharisees to various Torah texts. Throughout the Gospels we find Jesus offering interpretations of the Scriptures, which were quite similar to those of the Pharisees.

Finally, the Christian Scriptures provide us with plenty of examples of how deeply Jesus embraced the table fellowship of Pharisaism. The meal narratives in the Christian Scriptures are an example of this. In the end, Jesus selected this setting—table fellowship—for one of the most critical moments of his entire ministry, the celebration of what the Christian community has traditionally called the first Eucharist (see Matthew 26:26-30; Mark 14:22-26; Luke 22:14-20).

## The New Testament and the Pharisees

Readers of the Christian Scriptures are familiar with sections of the Gospels, especially in Matthew, in which the Pharisees appear as the arch-enemies of Jesus as well as opponents to his teaching and preaching. How, then, do we maintain a positive connection between the teachings of Jesus and those of the Pharisees?

Recall that Jesus' relations with the Pharisees were not always adversarial. Pharisees warned Jesus of the risks he was taking by his preaching and teaching (see Luke 13:31). Jesus praised some Pharisees, for example, "the scribe" of Mark 12:32; Jesus ate with Pharisees (Luke 7:36; 14:1).

There is, however, conflict between Jesus and the Pharisees in the Gospels. Understanding its sources can put things into a more positive perspective. Scholars suggest three possible approaches to this conflict.

The first approach sees Jesus and his teachings as quite similar to those of the Pharisees. The animosity in the Gospels, however, is the result of the interpretations of Jesus' actions that conflicted with those of the Pharisees. For example, Jesus' healing on the Sabbath and his disciples' picking grain on the Sabbath were actions clearly not supported by the Pharisees.

Another possible explanation for the Gospels' hostility toward the Pharisees results from our enhanced understanding of the Talmud, which is the collected teachings of the Pharisees and their rabbinic heirs. In the Talmud, we find reference to some seven categories of Pharisees, five viewed negatively, while the other two receive a positive evaluation. This list clearly shows us that the movement encompassed a wide range of viewpoints and, more important, that heated internal disputes were quite common. Considering this point, one could argue that the Gospel portraits of Jesus disputing with the "Pharisees" were the "hot debates" that were common in Pharisaic circles rather than true condemnations of Pharisaism.

A third scholarly approach stresses positive connections

between Jesus' central teachings and those of the Pharisees. These evident connections raise suspicions about the conflict texts. Surely Jesus would not denounce a movement with which he had so much in common. Therefore, either he was speaking in a very limited context or the conflict stories represent the situation in the latter part of the first century when the Gospels were written, rather than representing Jesus' own historical situation.

By the last third of the first century, the Christian community—now formally expelled from the synagogue— was engaged in intense competition with Jews for converts. The New Testament statements about conflict between Jesus and the Pharisees may reflect that competition. In sum, the Gospel conflict statements between Jesus and the Pharisees are most likely not those of the historical Jesus but instead those of the early Church, which wrote the Gospels.

## Jesus' Love of Scripture

Jesus' Bible was the Hebrew Scriptures, which in his day contained the Law and the Prophets. He not only read it, he was nurtured by it. We can sum up Jesus' attitude toward these sacred writings with his assertion, "Do not think that I have come to abolish the law or the prophets; I have come not to abolish but to fulfill" (Matthew 5:17).

Jesus' teachings, his anticipation, his hopes were all rooted in the Hebrew Scriptures. He would be unintelligible without them. All Jesus' teachings were either literally biblical, filtered through the Pharisaic use of Scripture or both.

In the Gospels Jesus often argued his position by using so-called "proof texts," quoting from the Hebrew Scriptures to prove a point or to refute a critic (see the Sermon on the Mount, Matthew 5—7). Jesus, as the Gospel writers presented him, drew on a technique used by the Pharisees.

Proof-texting at times pitted Jesus against the Pharisees— as when he challenged certain claims they made about the unwritten law and called them hypocrites for placing higher value on the teachings of humans than of God (Matthew 23:1-

36). Another example of this challenge is when he used Scripture to refute the Pharisaic teachings about plucking grain on the sabbath (Matthew 12:1-8) or eating with unwashed hands (Matthew 15:20).

At other times proof-texting placed Jesus on the side of the Pharisees. In an impressive debate with the Sadducees, he used the Hebrew Scriptures to reinforce his belief (and that of the Pharisees) in an afterlife. Jesus was so impressive he won the applause of the Pharisees (see Matthew 22:23-33).

Possibly the best example we have of Jesus' use of the Hebrew Scriptures is his teaching on love (see Matthew 22:34-40; Mark 12:28-34; Luke 10:25-28). A Pharisee asked him what commandment in the law is the greatest. Jesus responded by quoting Deuteronomy 6. "'You shall love the Lord your God with all your heart, and with all your soul, and with all your mind.' This is the greatest and first commandment" (Matthew 22:37-38). Jesus went on to say, "And a second is like it: 'You shall love your neighbor as yourself'" (Matthew 22:39; see Leviticus 19:18). In brief, Jesus was proof-texting his answer by quoting from the Hebrew Scriptures.

According to the Gospels, Jesus said that the entire law and the prophets are fulfilled in the saying, "Do to others as you would have them do to you" (Luke 6:31; see also Matthew 7:12). How does that fulfill the entire law? Just the way it did when someone asked Hillel, a Pharisaic sage, "Can you summarize the whole Torah (Law) while I stand on one foot?" Hillel said, "Do not do unto others as you would not have them do unto you, the rest is commentary. Go and learn it." Jesus maintained that there are two great commandments: Love God and love your neighbor. On both points he would have found widespread support among the Jewish teachers of his day, who also used such proverbs.

In brief, Jesus' use of the Hebrew Scriptures was unabashedly Jewish and was similar to that of his contemporaries, especially the Pharisees.

## Jesus and Jewish Feasts and Festivals

No treatment of the Jewishness of Jesus would be complete without looking at the feasts and festivals Jesus celebrated. During Jesus' time and beyond, Jews went to the Temple in Jerusalem and to the synagogues in and outside Palestine to celebrate births, weddings, deaths, national triumphs and tragedies—just as Christians do in our churches today.

Because the contemporary Jewish community celebrates Hanukkah around the same time we Christians celebrate Christmas, it seems appropriate to look at that feast first. Although Jesus never heard of Christmas, he was most likely familiar with Hanukkah and may have taken part in it as a child. Our imagination may allow us to see Mary or Joseph lighting the candles of the menorah for eight nights in their home in Nazareth. Imagine Joseph recounting the story of Judas Maccabeus and the marvelous events of 171 B.C.E. surrounding the recapture of the Temple, the center of Jewish life and worship. Hanukkah celebrates not only the centrality of the Jerusalem Temple, but also the national triumph restoring the Temple as the center of Jewish life and worship.

On December 25, 168 B.C.E., the Seleucid King Antiochus IV profaned the Temple in Jerusalem, erected an altar of sacrifice there to the pagan god Zeus and forbade Jews to practice their religion. Three years later, on the same date, Judas Maccabeus regained and purified the Temple, and apparently started a memorial celebration of this purification. The celebration, which lasted for eight days included reciting of the *Hallel* (Psalms 113-118) and processions with "green branches and palms" (2 Maccabees 10:7).

The distinctive feature of this celebration memorializes rekindling the Temple candelabra. The Jews lit olive oil lamps in front of their homes each night during the festival. One was lit the first day, two the second and another each day until all eight were lit.

The origins of this custom, according to rabbinic legend, stem from the fact that Judas Maccabeus found only one jar of holy oil in the Temple—a one-day supply for the candelabra. Miraculously, the oil lasted until more could be prepared eight days later. In Jewish homes today, one candle on the eight-branch menorah is lit the first night, and another added each night until all are lit. What today we know as the Feast of Lights or Hanukkah in Jesus' day was known as the Feast of the Dedication of the Temple (see John 10:22-42).

Mary and Joseph took Jesus to the Temple when he was barely a month old "to present him to the Lord" in fulfillment of the Mosaic Law (see Luke 2:22). From that moment on, the Temple played a key role in Jesus' life and in the life of his disciples, just as it did in the lives of all the Jewish people.

As Christians, we have taken over and freely applied the term "temple" to the Mystical Body of Christ, the communion of saints, the people of God in the Church. Similarly, we are familiar with the symbolism of lighted candles. Our present Advent wreath is reminiscent of the Hanukkah celebration of lights. The dedication of our houses to God is rooted in Jewish tradition and reverence for the Temple.

## The Jewish Liturgical Calendar and Jesus

The Hebrew people had a keen sense of the passage of time, both cyclic and linear. Because they were so dependent on land, crops and herds for their livelihood, they appreciated the cycles of nature more intimately than we moderns do. At the same time, more so than any of their contemporaries, the Jews were keenly aware that they were a community with a history that led away from the past, a people uniquely chosen by their God.

Three of the oldest feasts that Jesus most likely celebrated are harvest-related. Passover or *Pesach* fell during the barley harvest (March-April); Pentecost or *Shavuot* during the wheat harvest (June), and Tabernacles (Tents) or *Sukkot* during the fruit harvest (September-October). The specific dates for the celebration of these agricultural feasts were not fixed, but varied with geographical location and the length of the growing season.

These yearly agricultural celebrations were eventually connected with key events in Israel's history: the Exodus from Egypt (Passover), the giving of the Torah to Moses on Sinai (Pentecost) and wandering in the desert before entering the Promised Land (Tabernacles/Tents). From these events, in turn, emerged the central themes that occur repeatedly in the Jewish liturgies: redemption, revelation and creation. Like road signs, these three themes guide us as we walk through the Jewish feasts Jesus knew.

## Jesus and Passover: Redemption

It is not difficult to imagine Jesus as a young child asking the ritual Passover question, "Why is this night different from all other nights?" and listening intensely as his elders retold the story of his ancestors' redemption from slavery.

By the time he was a teenager, Jesus knew the background of the first major festival in the Jewish calendar, Passover (*Pesach*) (see Luke 2:41-42). Just as a Christian child today knows the dates of Christmas and Easter, so Jesus would have known that Jews celebrate Passover at twilight on the fourteenth of Nisan, the first month of the year. As it has come down to us from the days of Judah's King Josiah (640-609 B.C.E.), Pesach is a combination of a shepherd festival (the slaughtering and eating of the Paschal animal) and a week-long *matzot* festival (eating of unleavened bread), which coincided with the barley harvest. The people made the newly-harvested grain into bread without leaven, symbolizing a fresh beginning. One description of the festival and its connection with the liberation of the Jews from slavery appears in Exodus 12:1-28.

Passover is fittingly the first festival of the year because it is the Exodus, the redemption of the Jews from slavery in Egypt, which sets them apart and establishes their identity. That is as true of Jews today as it was of the first Hebrews who crossed the Red Sea to freedom. As one contemporary Jewish writer puts it, "To be a Jew means to be a slave who has been liberated by God."

Everything about the celebration of Passover is designed to

enable all Jews to experience for themselves the suffering of slavery and the embracing of freedom, but it is particularly structured with the education of the children in mind. The Seder, or ritual meal, consists of special symbolic foods: bitter herbs dipped in salt water (reminiscent of the sweat and tears of the people in bondage); matzot (unleavened bread) and a lamb shank (recalling the paschal animal); a narration known in Hebrew as *Haggadah* (retelling the story of the Exodus), psalms, prayers and songs. The youngest child asks four questions about the significance of the Seder and, playfully in some homes, all of the children try to catch the leader of the service drinking from the cup of wine reserved for Elijah.

It was most likely a Passover meal that Jesus celebrated before his passion, death and resurrection. Jesus raised one of the four Passover cups of wine when he said, "This cup that is poured out for you is the new covenant in my blood" (Luke 22:20).

The early Church applied the rich symbolism of Passover to the person of Jesus. The book of Revelation describes him as the Paschal Lamb:

> Worthy is the Lamb that was slaughtered
> to receive power and wealth and wisdom and might
> and honor and glory and blessing! (Revelation 5:12)

### Jesus and the Feast of Pentecost: Revelation

If Passover gave Jesus a sense of history and identity, answering for him the question, "Who are we?" the next major festival, Pentecost, answered the question, "Why were we freed from bondage in Egypt?"

During the second night of Passover, Jesus would have begun counting the fifty days until the next festival, Pentecost (Shavuot). Jews saw this feast as coinciding with the Hebrews' arrival at Sinai, the establishment of the covenant and the giving of the Torah to Moses. Just as Passover celebrates the Jews' freedom from slavery, Pentecost celebrates their freedom for a life of faithfulness to the Torah. Passover and Pentecost are two sides of the same coin. Redemption occurred for the sake of revelation, so that Israel might be a kingdom of priests, a holy nation.

As with other harvest festivals, Pentecost would have been an occasion for Jesus and all male Jews to make a required pilgrimage to the Temple for the prescribed offering. Imagine the press of the crowds, the odors of the gifts burning on the altar and the excitement in the air as Jews from outlying regions converged on the holy city of Jerusalem. It is no accident then that Luke describes the descent of the Holy Spirit as taking place during Shavuot/Pentecost (see Acts 2:1-13). He presents Jesus as the new Moses, the one who ascended to the right hand of the Father and sent the Holy Spirit, thus establishing the new covenant and its law of love.

Jesus may have spent part of this Pentecost festival day in a synagogue in the company of other religious leaders and ordinary Jews discussing Exodus 19—24, the story of the events at Sinai. In some synagogues today, a section of the Book of Ruth is also read. It is the story of the Moabite ancestor of Jesus who freely placed herself under the covenant of Sinai:

> Where you go, I will go;
> Where you lodge, I will lodge;
> your people shall be my people,
> and your God my God (Ruth 1:16d).

As the Gospel of Matthew maintains, Jesus came not to abolish the law, but to fulfill it (see Matthew 5:17). The Jewish and Christian Pentecosts celebrate the two revelations of the one God—Torah for Jews, Jesus for Christians. By word and example, Jesus taught that faithfulness to the oral and written Torah results in a righteous way of life. Rabbis after him taught that the Torah preceded the creation of the world. It was for the sake of the Torah that God created and redeemed the Jew. Torah gives life.

### Jesus and the Feast of Tabernacles (Tents): Creation

In the third of the harvest feasts, Jesus would have looked back to the very beginning of time—the creation of the world—and celebrated the gifts of the land. The one-day spring festival of Pentecost paled in comparison to the week-long fall festival, the Feast of Tents (Sukkot). When the crops were all gathered in, the people journeyed to Jerusalem to celebrate the abundance of the land, the wonders of creation and the goodness of God. Besides the religious ceremonies, the days had an atmosphere comparable to an Oktoberfest. The joyousness of the festival is no doubt due to the harvest and to the fact that it falls five days after the solemn period marked by the Day of Atonement.

The Feast of Tents (Tabernacles) probably derives its name from the practice of building temporary shelters in the fields and vineyards to provide the harvesters some protection from the elements.

The "tents" the Jews constructed for the festival were more along the line of carnival booths or shelters put up for an outdoor meeting rather than modern camping gear. Eventually, the practice of building the shelters in the Temple precincts was tied to the days before the Jews entered the Promised Land, when they lived in the desert without fixed abodes.

The Book of Numbers describes the various sacrifices offered on each day of the Feast of Tents—some seventy in all. Besides the sacrifices, Jews celebrated two distinctive rituals during the course of the week. In the first ritual, each worshiper carried an *esrog* (a lemon-like fruit) and a palm branch to which were tied myrtle and willow twigs. When verses of Psalm 118 were pronounced during the Temple service, the people waved the palm branches in unison.

The second ritual consisted of a libation of water followed by a procession with lights. According to tradition, the water was brought in a golden flask from the fountain of Siloam. The officiating *kohen* (priest) poured it into the basin near the altar. A torchlight procession, dances, singing and most likely the chanting of the psalms of ascents (Psalms 120—134) to the accompaniment of musical instruments accompanied the ceremony.

According to John 7:37b-38, it was during the Feast of Tents that Jesus said "Let anyone who is thirsty come to me, and let the one who believes in me drink. As the scripture has said, 'Out of the believer's heart shall flow rivers of living water.'" Later we read, "Again Jesus spoke to them, saying, 'I am the light of the world. Whoever follows me will never walk in darkness but will have the light of life'" (John 8:12). It would have been obvious to Jesus' listeners that he was making his own the rich symbols of water and light connected with the Feast of Tents.

## Yom Kippur and Jesus

We now turn to the period known as the High Holy Days, a most solemn occasion. In the modern Jewish calendar this penitential period, also known as the Days of Awe, begins with Rosh Hashanah ("head of the year" or new year) and concludes ten days later with Yom Kippur (Day of Atonement).

Yom Kippur is ultimately a celebration of hope—of belief in God's forgiveness and the ability of humans to change— although it deals with such weighty themes as death, sin, judgment and repentance. Originally, Rosh Hashanah is a special new moon festival commemorating the New Year according to a calendar that was no longer in use by the time of Jesus. It is uncertain whether Jesus took part in this now-popular celebration.

There is no doubt, however, that he was familiar with it. As he was growing up, Jesus may have witnessed the Yom Kippur ritual of the scapegoat. The high priest symbolically transferred the sins of the people to the animal by laying his hands on it before it was slaughtered or driven out into the desert.

Little wonder, then, that some of his listeners accused Jesus of blasphemy when he said to the paralyzed man, "Son, your sins are forgiven" (Mark 2:5b). Jesus not only forgave sins, but in the end he also offered himself as the unblemished victim for our sins. Christians can explore this imagery as applied to Jesus by reading the Letter to the Hebrews.

For Christians, no less than for Jews, the major feasts of Hanukkah, Yom Kippur, Passover, Pentecost and Tabernacles provide opportunities to explore further the rich spiritual heritage we share. As Christians, some of our liturgical feasts and festivals have their roots in those of Judaism, our family of origin in faith.

## Appreciating Judaism

What will befriending Jesus the Jew mean in our local parish community and in our own lives? Will it combat ignorance or misperceptions about Jesus? Will it mean revising our suspicions about our Jewish brothers and sisters? Will an awareness of Jesus as Jewish cause us to examine any compulsion we may have to convert Jews or condemn them? Will the Jewish roots of Jesus help us to better understand our own faith and that of contemporary Jews? Will we remember when we celebrate the liturgy that its roots are in the synagogue and Jewish ritual?

### For Discussion

1) *If you had to convince a friend that this chapter changed your attitude toward Jesus' origins and toward Jews today, what would you say?*

2) *What example of Jesus making use of the Hebrew Scriptures means the most to you? Why?*

3) *Why do you think there is so much hostility in the Gospels toward the Pharisees?*

4) *How do the feasts and festivals that Jesus celebrated help you better understand the liturgy of the Church?*

### For Further Reading

DiSante, Carmine. *Jewish Prayer: The Origins of Christian Liturgy*. Mahwah, N.J.: Paulist Press, 1991.

Guignebert, Charles. *The Jewish World in the Time of Jesus*. New York: University Press, 1979.

Koenig, John. *Jews and Christians in Dialogue: New Testament Foundations.* Philadelphia: Westminster, 1979.

Lee, Bernard L. *The Galilean Jewishness of Jesus.* Mahwah, N.J.: Paulist Press, 1988.

Murphy, Frederick J. *The Religious World of Jesus.* Nashville: Abingdon, 1991.

Shermis, Michael, and Arthur E. Zannoni, eds. *Introduction to Jewish-Christian Relations.* Mahwah, N.J.: Paulist Press, 1991.

Swidler, Leonard. *Yeshua: A Model for Moderns.* Kansas City, Mo.: Sheed and Ward, 1988.

Vermes, Geza. *Jesus and the World of Judaism.* Philadelphia: Fortress Press, 1983.

_____. *Jesus the Jew: A Historian's Reading of the Gospels.* New York: Macmillan, 1973.

_____. *The Religion of Jesus the Jew.* Minneapolis, Minn.: Fortress Press, 1993.

Zannoni, Arthur E., ed. *Jews and Christians Speak of Jesus.* Minneapolis, Minn.: Fortress Press, 1994.

CHAPTER THREE

# Gospel Titles for Jesus

D id you ever have someone ask you what other people thought of you or who they thought you were? Such a question would make most of us feel a little uncomfortable and awkward. After all, people do not usually go around asking such questions, let alone seeking an answer.

Such feelings may have gone through the minds of the disciples when Jesus asked them: "Who do people say that I am?" (Mark 8:27b). The disciples seem a little awkward in their response, for they recite a whole litany: John the Baptist, Elijah, one of the prophets (see Mark 8:28). These responses imply a wide variety of views among Jesus' contemporaries.

Varying views of Jesus are found throughout the Christian Scriptures, especially in the Gospels. The evangelists knew that the meaning of who Jesus was and what he did could not be "captured" by one title, so they used a variety of titles when speaking about him. Some probably originated in Jesus' lifetime—Messiah or Christ, Son of Man, Savior and Prophet. Others, however, may be the result of reflections by the early Christian community, the Church, on the experience of salvation in and through Christ: Lord, Servant, Son of God, High Priest, Word, Wisdom of God, Son of David, Lamb of God.

In this chapter we will explore these titles and how people applied them to Jesus. We will arrive at a better response to the question and a new respect for the writers of the Christian Scriptures, who knew that no one person can ever be summed up by a single label. Our own lives and their meaning cannot be reduced to our titles—brother, sister, son, daughter, mother, father, husband, wife, employer, employee, dentist, doctor, nurse, engineer, lawyer, teacher, pharmacist. Neither can Jesus and his life.

## Jesus

This is not a title but the name the angel told Joseph to give the child Mary conceived by the power of the Holy Spirit. In Hebrew *Yeshua*, in Greek, *Jesous*, the name means "the Lord [Yahweh] saves."

Why such a name? Because, as the angel in Matthew's Gospel tells Joseph: "...he will save his people from their sins" (Matthew 1:21b).

## Messiah or Christ

Christ is not Jesus' last name. Greeks used the title *Christos* to translate the Hebrew term *Messiah*, "anointed one." The Hebrew Scriptures used the title to designate the king, for kings were anointed often by one of God's prophets (Saul and David were both anointed by the prophet Samuel). Just as the olive oil used in anointing penetrated the skin, so to the ancient mind did God's Spirit penetrate the individual being anointed.

The Gospels understood Jesus as completely penetrated with God's Spirit. "Christ" or "anointed one" was the title given to Jesus at an early stage in the Church's preaching. It signified the early Church's understanding that Jesus was the expected one and that in him a new age had begun. After the Resurrection Peter could proclaim Jesus as truly God's Messiah, "Therefore let the entire house of Israel know with certainty that God has made him both Lord and Messiah, this Jesus whom you crucified" (Acts 2:36).

## Son of Man

The term *Son of Man* comes from the Hebrew *ben'adam* or the Aramaic *bar anash*. The normal translation for these terms is "human being." The title has a double origin in the Hebrew

42

Scriptures. In the Book of Ezekiel, God addresses the prophet with this title in order to contrast the mortal humanity of the prophet, God's messenger, with the immortal divinity of the one God who is giving the message. The Psalms and the Book of Job use the term similarly (see Psalms 8:4; 80:17; Job 25:6).

In the Book of Daniel, the title appears in a different sense and with a different usage. Daniel 7:13-14 speaks of one "like a human being" ("Son of Man") who approaches the throne of the "Ancient of Days."

The Book of Daniel, however, is a type of writing known as apocalyptic. In this type of literature, humans represent divine beings. The "Son of Man," following the interpretation given in Daniel, is a superhuman being who represents the nation, Israel (see Daniel 7:17-18, 27). Later Jewish literature applied this title to the judge who would appear at the end of time (see, for example, Matthew 25).

In the Gospels, only Jesus uses "Son of Man" to refer to himself. We can classify this usage in three categories. The first group includes sayings where Jesus speaks in the first person: the earthly Son of Man sayings (see, for example, Matthew 11:18-19). The second group consists of the suffering Son of Man sayings where Jesus explicitly speaks of his passion (such as Mark 9:31). The final group is the eschatological (endtime) Son of Man sayings where the influence of the Book of Daniel is most prominent (as in Mark 8:38).

In sum, when the Gospel writers apply the title *Son of Man* to Jesus they mean either a human being or the final endtime character who will come to judge the living and the dead. Context often decides the meaning. For example, in Mark 9:31, Jesus teaches the disciples that "[t]he Son of Man is to be betrayed into human hands, and they will kill him, and three days after being killed, he will rise again." Matthew 25:31-46, on the other hand, portrays the Son of Man as the judge who will come at the end of time to separate the sheep from the goats and decide who will enter the Kingdom.

## Savior

The Christian Scriptures frequently speak of salvation and of Jesus as Savior. Jesus preaches salvation by proclaiming the Kingdom of God. Through Jesus, God has established a communion with God's people, which means now they are saved. The Gospel itself is the message of salvation: "...to us the message of this salvation has been sent" (Acts 13:26).

The authors of the Gospels present Jesus as the one who offered salvation. Angels proclaimed it to the shepherds (see Luke 2:10-11). Jesus himself extended it to all who would listen: the upright and the sinner, the rich and the poor. Jesus broke the power of evil. No longer might people think of history's outcome as good or bad. Goodness is the only response. God established an irrevocable communion with humankind.

As savior, Jesus was concerned principally with the healing of the soul, the spiritual dimension of human life. Jesus saved people from sin and helped them to overcome their evil tendencies. Jesus, in his lifetime, told people to sin no more; he continues to echo this refrain throughout human history. The soul, the spirit, needs the saving presence of God. Jesus responded by giving people a sense of fulfillment in their spiritual lives. They could turn their backs on a life of sin and walk away from the darkness of evil into the light of goodness and truth. This challenge Jesus still gives to all of his followers.

## Prophet

As a prophet, Jesus was a spokesperson for God. He followed in the footsteps of the great prophets of the Hebrew Scriptures—Isaiah, Jeremiah, Ezekiel. In the Gospels, the title *prophet* is often applied to Jesus by the crowds as their response to his actions (see, for example, Matthew 21:11). At Jesus' trial, his critics abuse him and call upon him to "prophesy" (Mark 14:65; Luke 22:64): Even his enemies evaluated him as a prophet.

Jesus apparently considered himself a prophet. In the synagogue at Nazareth, he seems to identify himself and his mission of liberation with that of Isaiah the prophet: "The spirit of the Lord is upon me,/because he has anointed me/to bring good news to the poor" (Luke 4:16-21; see Isaiah 61:1-2). When people challenge his authority in Nazareth, Jesus makes the well-known remark, "Prophets are not without honor, except in their hometown, and among their own kin, and in their own house" (Mark 6:4).

The Gospels often portray Jesus as aware that he shares the fate of those prophets who were killed by people who would not accept them as messengers of God. Nowhere is this more vividly articulated than in Jesus' lament over Jerusalem: "Jerusalem, Jerusalem, the city that kills the prophets and stones those who are sent to it! How often have I desired to gather your children together as a hen gathers her brood under her wings, and you were not willing!" (Luke 13:34).

The Gospels also interpret Jesus as the long-awaited prophet promised to Moses (see Deuteronomy 18:15-18). In his day, Jesus' contemporaries had developed a hope for an eschatological (endtime) prophet. Both John the Baptist (John 1:21) and Jesus (John 6:14; 7:40) were thought perhaps to be such a prophet. The primary role of this prophet was to inaugurate the endtime. This "time" was not the end of the world, but the era when one would see the radical inbreaking of the Reign of God into the world and into the hearts and minds of humans.

Jesus' role as prophet has a real bearing on our practice of faith. At Baptism, we were incorporated into the priestly, kingly and prophetic ministry of Jesus. If we take our baptismal promises seriously, we, too, are called, like Jesus, to believe that the Spirit of the Lord is upon us, empowering us to be spokespersons for God; people of faith who believe in the radical inbreaking of the Reign of God—people who criticize the oppression of the poor, the foreigner, the minority member, the abused; those who seek justice for the marginalized; those who proclaim freedom for captives—a people whose life-style is changed by the Gospels.

To be prophetic today means exposing the values of our culture to criticism, just as Jesus did, challenging what we believe or are taught to believe by the government, the media and our consumerist society. This prophetic dimension of our faith calls us to be countercultural voices in the wilderness, preparing the way for God's reign, where not only the lion will lie down with the lamb, but the elderly will be cared for by the young; the poor and rich will eat together; and the proud and haughty will be brought low. As faithful followers of Jesus, we are called to be prophets, for

> Surely the Lord GOD does nothing,
>    without revealing his secret
>    to his servants the prophets (Amos 3:7).

## Lord

In the Book of Exodus, God reveals himself to Moses at the burning bush and agrees to Moses' request for the divine name. In its original formulation, the name consisted of four Hebrew consonants: *YHWH*. This was the proper name for God. When, approximately two centuries before Jesus lived, the Hebrew Scriptures were translated by seventy sages into Greek (the Septuagint), the name was translated by the Greek word *kyrios*, "Lord." The word was the strongest way of asserting in the Greek language the true divinity of Israel's God. In brief, *kyrios*, "Lord," is the Greek equivalent of God's very name.

The Christian Scriptures use the name *Lord* to refer to God and as a description for Jesus. The name expresses Jesus' post-Resurrection status. Due to his victory over death, he is the supreme Lord of life and death. The title proclaims Jesus' divine sovereignty.

An early Christian profession of faith was "Jesus is Lord!" For Paul, writing to the Corinthians, such an act of faith required the power of the Holy Spirit: "[N]o one can say 'Jesus is Lord' except by the Holy Spirit" (1 Corinthians 12:3). The Book of Revelation, the final book of the Christian Scriptures, closes with the prayer, "Come, Lord Jesus!"

(Revelation 22:20).

Interestingly, the early Church developed in the Roman Empire, where citizens called Caesar "Lord." Christians could never apply this title to the emperor.

## Servant

"Servant of God" originates in the Suffering Servant canticles (songs) of Second Isaiah (Isaiah 42:1-9; 49:1-7; 50:4-11; 52:13—53:12). The second poem depicts this servant as one who vicariously suffers for the people. When the early Church began to reflect on the sufferings of Jesus and sought justification for it in the Jewish Scriptures, they immediately turned to that Isaian canticle, which stressed the atoning value of suffering. It struck the early preachers of the Church as a clear and concise explanation of the mission of Jesus, both then and throughout the history of God's people. Jesus suffered to die and atone for the wrongs of God's people, fulfilling the role portrayed by Isaiah. This conviction is conveyed quite clearly in Matthew 12:18-21, which quotes from the first servant song (Isaiah 42:1-4) to describe Jesus.

## Son of God

The Hebrew Scriptures applied the term *Son of God* to the people of Israel and to their kings. In those contexts the term did not imply divinity, but meant God's adoption of the people and the king that brought them into an intimate relationship with God.

When the Christian Scriptures call Jesus Son of God, it is a post-Resurrection interpretation by the early Church. Mark's Gospel, for example, reinterprets the title to fit its primary focus of suffering. The high point of the Gospel comes when the centurion recognizes the crucified body of Jesus as the Son of God (Mark 15:39).

Mark identifies Jesus as the Son of God and then defines the title in terms of the Suffering Servant. Paul, on the other hand, maintains that Jesus "...was declared to be Son of God with power according to the spirit of holiness by resurrection from the dead..." (Romans 1:4). And the Gospel of John confidently proclaims, "...and we have seen his glory, the glory as of a father's only son, full of grace and truth" (John 1:14b).

## High Priest

The early Jewish-Christians envisioned Jesus as the eternal high priest. (The result of their reflection is the Epistle to the Hebrews.) The major use of the title in the Hebrew Scriptures is for the high priest of the temple of Jerusalem, who offered sacrifice and acted on behalf of the people, especially on the Day of Atonement.

The title suggests a further allusion: In Genesis 14 an interesting character appears, the priest-king Melchizedek. He brings out bread and wine, blesses Abraham and vanishes from the narrative.

Melchizedek reappears in Psalm 110:4, a royal coronation psalm that declares the king being enthroned is a priest in the line of the priest-king Melchizedek. It also provides the possibility for a link between priesthood and messiahship.

In Hebrews 7, the priest of Melchizedek's line has an eternal priesthood. He enters once and for all to perform the final sacrifice. The repeated sacrifices of the high priests in the Temple are no longer necessary. Jesus is that eternal high priest who has acted definitively.

## Word

John 1:1-14 applies the title *Word*, *Logos* in Greek, to Jesus. John views the *Logos* as preexistent and divine. The ultimate point of the Prologue, however, is neither preexistence, nor divinity, but verse 14: "And the Word became flesh and lived among us, and we have seen his glory, the glory as of a father's only son...." The climax of the hymn is not the relationship between the *Logos* and flesh. The verb *became* announces a change in the mode of being of the *Logos*: before he was in the glory of God; now he has taken on the lowliness of human existence.

In Johannine terms, the word flesh (*sarkx*) is not just another way of expressing a human being. Flesh means the earthbound, as seen in John 3:6; it connotes something transient and perishable, as in John 6:63. Flesh is the typical mode of being human in contrast to the divine and spiritual.

Once the *logos* has become flesh in the Prologue of John's Gospel, no further use of the title appears in the rest of the Fourth Gospel. This Gospel contains a fully developed theology of the word of God. Now we are dealing with not the eternal *logos* in the bosom of the Father, but the Word that has become flesh—human—in Jesus of Nazareth. *Logos* emphasizes the divinity of Jesus. But because the Word is enfleshed, the title also includes the humanity of Jesus.

## Wisdom of God

Another image for Jesus found in the Christian Scriptures relates him quite intimately to the wisdom of God. In Jewish wisdom literature (especially Proverbs, Job, Ecclesiastes, Sirach and the Book of Wisdom), wisdom is often personified as "Lady Wisdom." Consistent with this personification, *wisdom* is a female noun in both Hebrew (*hokmah*) and Greek (*sophia*). In the opening chapter of the Book of Proverbs, Lady Wisdom, Sophia, speaks in a public place like a biblical prophet (see Proverbs 1:20-33). Her various roles are more clearly described in an extended speech in Proverbs 8:1-9:6, in which Sophia speaks of herself as the source of truth, insight and strength, as one who participated in God's creative work.

The Jewish personification of wisdom and the attribution to her of divine qualities becomes most developed in Sirach and Wisdom. In Sirach, Wisdom speaks of her origin in God "in the beginning":

> Before the ages, in the beginning, he [God] created me,
> and for all the ages I shall not cease to be (Sirach 24:9).

Wisdom speaks of her presence everywhere in Sirach 24, and

then the author refers to Sophia pitching her tent and dwelling in Israel. God "chose the place for my tent" (Sirach 24:8) among the people of Jacob, and she was in the tabernacle of the wilderness until she came to dwell in Jerusalem. She is identical with the divine presence.

The qualities of Lady Wisdom are most developed in the Book of Wisdom, written close to the time of Jesus. She is "the fashioner of all things" (Wisdom 7:22) and the "mother" of all good things (Wisdom 7:11-12), and is presented as having all the attributes of God. Thus, in the Book of Wisdom as a whole, wisdom has qualities and functions normally attributed to God.

Turning to the Christian Scriptures, there are many passages in the Gospels that associate Jesus with Wisdom. The Gospels present Jesus as saying: "Therefore also the Wisdom of God said, 'I will send them prophets and apostles, some of whom they will kill and persecute,' so that this generation may be charged with the blood of all the prophets shed since the foundation of the world" (Luke 11:49-50; see also Matthew 23:34-45).

What seems most important is the introductory phrase in which Jesus speaks for divine Wisdom. Speaking her words, he is the envoy or emissary of Dame Wisdom.

In another passage from Luke, Jesus speaks of himself as a child of Wisdom. At the end of a passage that reports vehement criticisms against both Jesus and John the Baptizer, Jesus says: "For John the Baptist has come eating no bread and drinking no wine, and you say, 'He has a demon'; the Son of Man has come eating and drinking, and you say, 'Look, a glutton and drunkard, a friend of tax collectors and sinners!' Nevertheless, wisdom is vindicated by all her children" (Luke 7:33-35).

Here Jesus speaks of himself (and by implication of John the Baptist) as a child of wisdom. Taken together, these two passages imply that the early Christian movement (the Church) saw Jesus as both spokesperson for and child of Wisdom.

The apostle Paul also uses Wisdom as a central category for describing Jesus. Paul speaks explicitly of Jesus as the Wisdom of God in the First Letter to the Corinthians: "...but we proclaim Christ crucified, a stumbling block to Jews and foolishness to Gentiles, but to those who are the called, both Jews and Greeks, Christ the power of God and the wisdom of God" (1 Corinthians 1:23-24).

A few lines later, Paul proclaims "[God] is the source of your life in Christ Jesus, who became for us wisdom from God..." (1 Corinthians 1:30a). Considering these passages, it seems Paul understood Jesus to be both the Wisdom *of* God and the wisdom *from* God.

There is another connection between Jewish language about Wisdom and Paul's language about Jesus. Paul speaks of Christ existing from eternity with God and taking an active part in creation. Paul's succinct formula states, "[Y]et for us there is one God, the Father, from whom are all things and for whom we exist, and one Lord, Jesus Christ, through whom are all things and through whom we exist" (1 Corinthians 8:6).

Paul expands on this description in a second passage describing Christ's role in creation: "He [Christ] is the image of the invisible God, the firstborn of all creation; for in him all things in heaven and on earth were created, things visible and invisible, whether thrones or dominions or rulers or powers— all things have been created through him and for him. He himself is before all things, and in him all things hold together" (Colossians 1:15-17).

The vocabulary here used about Christ is, of course, very similar to that used of Wisdom (*Sophia*) in the Jewish tradition that shaped Paul. It seems to not only describe Jesus in the language of divine Wisdom, but also to identify Jesus with Wisdom. For Paul, Jesus is the embodiment of the Wisdom of God.

## Son of David

Many Jews looked forward to a political, national and earthly

Messiah descended from King David (see 2 Samuel 7:12-16) who, by liberating and restoring them, would initiate the final age of salvation. In Mark's Gospel, Jesus is associated with this expectation by the blind Bartemeus, who cries out to him as "Son of David," begging for restored health (see Mark 10:46-52). The infancy narratives in Luke and Matthew present Jesus as a "son of David." When Jesus enters Jerusalem on a colt, he arouses the Davidic hopes of the crowds. They exclaim: "Blessed is the coming kingdom of our ancestor David!" (Mark 11:10).

Jesus fulfills the longing for a Davidic Messiah not as the expected political and earthly ruler, but as one who by suffering, dying and rising becomes the heavenly and exalted "Lord" seated at God's right hand, victorious over his enemies (see Mark 12:35-37).

## Lamb of God

John the Baptist twice hails Jesus with this title at the beginning of the Gospel of John (1:29, 35). The idea of the Lamb as a sacrificial offering lies behind these texts. In the Book of Revelation, the Lamb also appears several times as a symbol for Christ. There, the Lamb has clearly been slain as a ransom for sin. The Suffering Servant of Isaiah 53, who is presented as "a lamb that is led to the slaughter," possibly influenced this description of Jesus (see 1 Peter 1:18-19). In the Gospel of John, Jesus died on the afternoon before the Feast of Passover, as the Passover lambs were being slain in the Temple—thus presenting Jesus as the lamb of the Passover sacrifice. The designation of Jesus as the Lamb of God, then, suggests a wide range of images from the Hebrew Scriptures, mostly having to do with expiatory sacrifice.

## Conclusion

The varied portraits of Jesus found in the Gospels show us that Jesus, the central figure of our faith, defies a simple, one-dimensional analysis. The Gospels show us that there was much debate over who he was, what he said and how he affected those he encountered. Ultimately, we can only grasp the mystery of who Jesus is through the eyes of faith. Reflecting on his many titles can expand our images and understanding.

## For Discussion

*1) Why is it impossible to capture in any one title who Jesus was?*

*2) How has your understanding of Jesus changed as a result of exploring the various titles applied to him?*

*3) Are you more comfortable with some of the titles applied to Jesus in the Gospels than with others? Why?*

*4) How might this chapter help you in the practice of your faith?*

## For Further Reading

Borg, Marcus J. *Meeting Jesus Again for the First Time: The Historical Jesus and the Heart of Contemporary Faith.* San Francisco: Harper, 1994.

Cook, Michael L. *Responses to 101 Questions About Jesus.* Mahwah, N.J.: Paulist Press, 1993.

Fitzmyer, Joseph A. *A Christological Catechism: New Testament Answers (New Revised and Expanded Edition).* Mahwah, N.J.: Paulist Press, 1991.

McBride, Alfred. *Images of Jesus.* Cincinnati: St. Anthony Messenger Press, 1993.

Senior, Donald. *Jesus: A Gospel Portrait (Revised and Expanded Edition).* Mahwah, N.J.: Paulist Press, 1992.

Swidler, Leonard. *Yeshua: A Model for Moderns.* Kansas City, Mo.: Sheed & Ward, 1988.

CHAPTER FOUR

# The Kingdom (Reign) of God and Jesus

A ll of us are committed to causes: Little League baseball, scouting, recycling, United Way, Greenpeace, Amnesty International, Alcoholics Anonymous, Mothers Against Drunk Driving, a veteran's organization, or a service club. Jesus was also committed to a cause—one people knew as the Kingdom of God. Jesus lived, preached, witnessed and died on the cross in service of the Kingdom, and challenged his disciples to champion it as well.

In the Synoptic Gospels, the writers frequently introduce Jesus' teachings with the expression, "The Kingdom [or Reign] of God is like...." The very first words from the mouth of Jesus in the Gospel of Mark place the Kingdom at the core of Jesus' proclamation. "The time is fulfilled, and the kingdom of God has come near; repent, and believe in the good news" (Mark 1:15). *Repent* here means to give up the way you are living and start living for God. "The Kingdom" evokes images of God ruling over the people. We find such images throughout the Hebrew Scriptures, which often portray God as a just king whose reign is one of peace and justice. We Americans do not like people lording it over us, and we resent any attempt to remove our freedoms. Jesus and the Gospels ask us to change the way we are living.

For the people of ancient Israel, the Reign of God represented the time in which God would fulfill the divine promises, when God's people would worship from their hearts. It is the time Isaiah refers to when he says the lion and the calf will lie down together. It is the great banquet to which

55

all the nations will be called. The Kingdom (Reign) of God is the end of the reign of sin and death. For the Jews, God's reign signified the endtime, when God would act with justice on behalf of the people. In a sense, the Kingdom of God is a metaphor for God's presence, not only in the world but also in people.

When Jesus proclaimed the coming of the Reign of God, he was not inventing a new religious idea, but using one that appeared in the Hebrew Scriptures. The phrase *Reign* or *Kingdom of God* does not appear often in the Hebrew Scriptures, but we can tie its meaning to several different ideas. God's Reign is when humans submit to God's will. It is achieved through the power of God in relationship to the people Israel. It concerns God's judgment and God's establishment of Israel as the light to the Gentiles. God's Reign is related to the Day of the Lord, when God will reveal all the divine glory and judge all the nations of the earth.

In some parts of the Hebrew Scriptures, the Reign of God is a reality closely associated with this world. It will mean the end of war, pestilence and disease; it will bring material and political blessings. In other parts of the Scriptures, the idea seems more closely tied to an eschatological Kingdom: that is, a Kingdom that will close human history and begin where human history ends.

In view of these different ideas, when Jesus proclaimed the arrival of the Reign of God, the proclamation probably meant different things to different people. Jesus would infuse this phrase with his own meaning, for his understanding of the Kingdom was related to the past notion but was also distinct from it. At no point does Jesus formally spell out what he means by the Reign of God. He does not offer a theological treatise but a spiritual reality that an individual can only understand through the eyes of faith.

For some of Jesus' contemporaries the true experience of God's Reign could only come with the Messianic Age when evil had been destroyed, Israel was completely obedient to God and all nations would clearly see the Lord's presence as ruler of Israel.

In Jesus' preaching, the Kingdom is not just some distant future event. The Kingdom's presence shows in persons whose lives are changed. But the Kingdom, God's Reign, is not identical with what happens in this world. There is also, according to the Gospels, the future coming of the Kingdom at the end of time, when its promise of salvation and ultimate union with God is completely fulfilled. We can see this in Matthew 25, the Parable of the Last Judgment, and Mark 14:25, where Jesus says at the Last Supper, "...I will never again drink of the fruit of the vine until that day when I drink it new in the kingdom of God." Drinking anew with the Lord symbolizes the banquet of rejoicing in a new age to come.

Perhaps one of the more famous sayings of Jesus pointing to the presence of the Reign of God is in Luke 17:20-21:

> Once Jesus was asked by the Pharisees when the kingdom of God was coming, and he answered, "The kingdom of God is not coming with things that can be observed; nor will they say, 'Look, here it is!' or 'There it is!' For, in fact, the kingdom of God is among you."

This saying captured the imagination of the early followers of Jesus. Although Jesus had his disciples pray for the coming of the Kingdom in the Lord's Prayer, there is a clear Gospel tradition that he rejected all speculation about the exact time and place of its arrival. Rather, Jesus' disciples should learn to discern the presence of the Kingdom in their midst. In Luke 11:20, Jesus points to his exorcisms as one sign that the Kingdom is present. He also says that some of those present "...will not taste death before they see the kingdom of God" (Luke 9:27b). Jesus' contemporaries may have wondered if he meant that the final manifestation of the Reign of God, judgment and new creation, was right around the corner.

The Gospels maintain a healthy tension between the radical inbreaking of God's Reign here and now and the final coming of this Reign. They affirm both God's presence and the future outcome of this presence. It is a way of talking about God's simultaneous immanence and transcendence. In a sense, the Kingdom is a metaphor for this mystery.

Another way that Jesus proclaims the Reign of God is in

parables that are pointers for what it means to experience the Kingdom. Mark 4:11 speaks of the parables as revealing the "secret of the Kingdom of God." Further, persons who fail to grasp the parables are cut off from the Kingdom.

Some parables—the parable of the seed growing secretly (Mark 4:26-29) and the parable of the mustard seed (Mark 4:30-32), for example—envision the Kingdom by comparing it to a small, practically unnoticed seed. But when the seed is fully grown, there is a great harvest or a resting place for the birds. In this way, the Gospel writers show us that the Kingdom is *not* something that God alone causes with a dramatic, cosmic gesture, as the stories of the end of the world have it. Instead, the Kingdom may begin in a way that is almost invisible. The Kingdom is both event and process. While the Kingdom is the believer's goal, there is a whole process for attaining it. That process is revealed by who people are and how they act.

When Jesus talks about the Kingdom in the Gospels, he usually speaks about the kinds of persons who will enter it. In Mark 12:28-34, a scribe asks Jesus what is the greatest commandment. Jesus quickly summarizes the law by speaking of the obligation to worship only God, to love God with our whole being and to love our neighbor. The scribe agrees and repeats what Jesus has said. Jesus concludes by saying to the scribe, "You are not far from the Kingdom of God." So we have here one type of person who is close to the Kingdom. This person understands that the essentials of a truly religious life are love of God and neighbor. In brief, personal behavior constitutes admittance to the Kingdom. This is the whole theme of the great judgment in Matthew 25:31-46—giving food to the hungry, welcome to the stranger, clothing to the naked, care to the sick and company to the imprisoned. These actions are signs of the Reign of God.

Another famous saying of Jesus compared persons who would enter the Kingdom of God to children: "Truly I tell you, whoever does not receive the kingdom of God as a little child will never enter it" (Mark 10:15). In Matthew's Gospel, the disciples come to Jesus and ask, "'Who is the greatest in the kingdom of heaven?' He called a child, whom he put among them, and said, 'Truly I tell you, unless you change and become like children, you will never enter the kingdom of heaven. Whoever becomes humble like this child is the greatest in the kingdom of heaven. Whoever welcomes one such child in my name welcomes me'" (Matthew 18:1-5).

When Nicodemus came to Jesus to ask about the signs he has performed, Jesus answered him, "Very truly, I tell you, no one can see the kingdom of God without being born from above" (John 3:3).

These sayings suggest that a change is necessary for persons to become part of the Kingdom. Why does Jesus offer a child as the model for entering the Kingdom? Because in the ancient world and still today children are wonder-filled and the most vulnerable members of society. To enter the reign of God, you must become like a child, both filled with wonder about God and vulnerable before humankind. The world, of course, would declare such a posture folly, but not so God.

In a sense we can say that the Kingdom is the unifying focus of all that Jesus taught. We should not think that Jesus was teaching about many things and that one of these things was the Kingdom of God; rather, Jesus taught only one thing, the Kingdom of God, and everything he said and did should be related to that. Jesus is a messenger of the Kingdom, a child of the Kingdom, the vision-keeper of the Kingdom and the one who dies for the Kingdom. Jesus' only sovereign is God, and as a faithful child of God he is called to be as vulnerable as a child. As disciples of Jesus we are called to see in Jesus' vulnerability and in our own a revelation of the Kingdom.

The important question is, "What did Jesus mean by the Kingdom of God?" Our first response is that Jesus is not so much attempting to describe some thing or some geographical country like the kingdom of Jordan, either theoretically or concretely. Nor is he making a political statement. He is attempting to compare those who experience God reigning in their life to those who are not currently aware of God's Reign in theirs. A better way of posing the question would be, "What does it mean to experience God's reigning?" or "What does God's sovereignty look like in one's life?"

In the Gospels Jesus seems to pose a threefold response: (1) The Kingdom is near or within; (2) the Kingdom is personal and (3) the Kingdom comes by vulnerability. Before we go on to examine each of these, it is important to realize that Jesus' teachings about the Kingdom conflicted with the prevailing understanding among his contemporaries. For example, they did not think that vulnerability constituted admission to the Kingdom. In many ways, Jesus' contemporaries saw his teachings about the Kingdom as both countercultural and unorthodox, as do many people today. Egocentric people see themselves as the center of the universe, while theocentric people see God as the center. When God has become your center, you are not far from the Kingdom of God.

## The Kingdom Is Near or Within

Jesus teaching that the Kingdom of God "is among you" (see Luke 17:20-21) rejects the notion held by many of his Jewish contemporaries that one could look for signs to "figure God out" and predict God's ways. For Jesus, God cannot be figured out and predicted, for God's ways are inscrutable. God is always more. God is beyond human understanding and it is arrogant even to attempt to predict when and how God will bring in the Kingdom.

In addition, Jesus strongly emphasized that preoccupation with the future often distracts people from the fact that God is already acting as sovereign. God's Reign does not lie wholly in the future, but is present in the here and now; it is within us, among us. God reigns in the hearts and minds of men and women right now. Jesus emphasized the Kingdom's nearness, even its presence. Jesus was not proclaiming that God was about to end this world, but that God's reign is "Emmanuel," God with us. God tents in our midst.

For Jesus, God's Reign is already breaking through. Jesus describes God's Reign by using commonplace details from the lives of his listeners. What is the Reign of God? It is like yeast, or a seed, or a woman who loses a coin, or a man who finds a pearl, or a farmer who sows. For Jesus, the Reign of God is found in the ordinary. God's Reign does not burst into our lives from outside. Rather, we discover God dwelling within, quietly and persistently fermenting our very being and our every action. In a sense, the Kingdom is like one's soul: We believe it is in us, but we cannot see it.

## The Kingdom Is Personal

In Luke 11:20, Jesus proclaims another provocative Kingdom saying: "But if it is by the finger of God that I cast out the demons, then the kingdom of God has come to you." Here Jesus insists that his own exorcisms are a manifestation of God's kingly power. God is not only acting through Jesus, but whenever demons are being cast out and health and wholeness restored, there God is, acting as sovereign to save the people. God's Reign is not cosmic in the sense that all creation will stand still and acknowledge God as king in fear and trembling. It is personal in that individuals are released from demonic oppression—violence, consumerism, substance abuse or whatever—and recognize God's Kingdom. The Reign of God has come upon those who have been liberated from demonic possession, people who have faced the shadow side of their lives and surrendered to God's ability to extricate them from its clutches. Recognizing the demons in one's life and asking God to exorcise them is a way of participating in the Kingdom.

## The Kingdom Comes by Vulnerability

Another of Jesus' Kingdom sayings is, "From the days of John the Baptist until now the kingdom of heaven has suffered violence, and the violent take it by force" (Matthew 11:12). Jesus is saying that the Reign of God is vulnerable to human violence. God does not force the Kingdom by bringing it with power and might; God's reign is not coercive. It is dependent on human free will and choice, on the fragile turning of the human heart, which is always free. In reality, God suffers the violence of anyone who would plunder the Kingdom.

For most of Jesus' contemporaries, Jesus' focus on the present and not the future, the personal and not the cosmic nature of God's Kingdom becomes both an outrage and a blasphemy. The Gospel view is that the Kingdom of God is not the result of Jesus' mighty victory over Israel's enemies nor a triumph of power, but a vulnerable suffering that awaits the free turning of others in heart and mind to God. In Jesus' case, this vulnerability is manifest in his embracing of the cross.

Jesus' image of the Kingdom of God is radically different from its common usage in late Palestinian Judaism. Is it any wonder, then, that Jesus got into trouble with his contemporaries and that the Romans eventually executed him? He was in direct conflict with the ideological interpretation of the Kingdom of God that expected future, cosmic triumph. For most, "the Kingdom of God" referred to a future event that would definitely reverse the present Roman oppression, a final and cosmic intervention of God that would establish God's people Israel forever and ever, and cast its enemies into oblivion.

For Jesus and his followers, however, its meaning is more opaque: The Kingdom of God is an experience that delivers us from our own kingdoms, our own selfish regimes; it causes us to recognize that God reigns in creation, in history and in our lives. For Jesus, the Kingdom of God is already and always present ("with you," "among you"), but always tied to an experience of our own radical fragility and vulnerability— a sense that we cannot force things or magically have it our own way.

In sum, the Gospel writers try to portray that the Reign of God is brought about by the power of God, and as such is capable of growth and transformation far beyond human calculations. Further, the Reign of God is both a present and a future reality, not a reality that occurs only after death or at the end of time. God's reign ushers in love and offers peace and reconciliation. Jesus' association with sinners and outcasts manifests this.

Finally, God's Reign demands a decision from anyone who believes the Gospel and takes it seriously. The story of the Gospel is not only the story of God's grace; it is also the story of our response. The offer of God's invitation is meaningless if we are not open to it, if we are unwilling to respond to the offer. To be a member of the Kingdom is to be open to the constant process of God's presence and activity. Such openness embraces vulnerability.

Jesus proclaimed the Reign of God in word and in deed, by what he did, how he lived and what he said. He proclaimed the Kingdom in stories, through exorcisms and healings and in his table-fellowship. In all of these and in many other ways, however, none stands out as much as Jesus' use of parables. We turn to this topic in the next chapter.

### For Discussion

1) *How does God reign in your life? What does it mean to say God is your sovereign?*

2) *In what ways do your own personal demons get in the way of embracing the Reign of God in your heart and mind? Explain.*

3) *How does embracing your vulnerability help to establish the Kingdom of God? Explain.*

4) *As a result of reading this chapter, what is different about your understanding of the Reign of God?*

### For Further Reading

Beasley-Murray, G.R. *Jesus and the Kingdom of God*. Grand Rapids, Mich.: Eerdmans/Exeter: Paternoster, 1986.

Chilton, Bruce, ed. *The Kingdom of God*. Philadelphia: Fortress Press, 1984.

Chilton, Bruce, & J.I.H. McDonald. *Jesus and the Ethics of the Kingdom.* Grand Rapids, Mich.: Eerdmans, 1987.

Dodd, C.H. *The Parables of the Kingdom.* New York: Scribner, 1961.

Hiers, Richard. *The Kingdom of God in the Synoptic Tradition.* Gainesville, Fla.: University of Florida Press, 1970.

Perrin, Norman. *Jesus and the Language of the Kingdom.* Philadelphia: Fortress Press, 1976.

William, Wendell, ed. *The Kingdom of God in 20th Century Interpretation.* Peabody, Mass.: Hendrickson, 1987.

# CHAPTER FIVE

# Jesus the Storyteller

All of us love a good story. More than that, we love a good story told well by a skillful storyteller. I still remember my grandfather telling us about the "old country" and how he would come alive and twinkle as he told these stories. When I was in grade school, my third grade teacher told us stories from the Bible and about the saints. My imagination was forever taken captive by these stories. Years later, in college, a favorite professor continued that tradition for me and my fellow students, captivating our class every week as he began his lecture with a story. Some of my rabbi friends exchange stories with me that constantly kindle my imagination.

Stories are powerful tools for teachers. Jesus, an excellent teacher, knew that. The Gospels are full of the stories he told, stories he used to deliver the Good News. One could almost begin a Gospel about Jesus with the line, "Once upon a time, in a far-off country, there lived a great storyteller."

Jesus often employed a type of story called a parable. The word *parable* derives from two Greek words: *para*, meaning "beside," and *ballo*, meaning "to throw." In its root derivation, the word means something that is "thrown beside." When Jesus taught with parables, he illustrated ideas about the Kingdom of God by examples ("thrown beside") drawn from the everyday experiences of his hearers. He would begin: "The kingdom of God is like..." a fig tree, a pearl, a sower, a mustard seed, a king who goes on a journey. Parables are the recounting of a common incident from daily life in concise, figurative form to illustrate a spiritual truth. Put very simply, parables use the familiar to explain the unfamiliar. Put another way, a parable is simply a story with a religious meaning drawn from ordinary life, or a story with a moral.

We find the parables of Jesus almost exclusively in the Synoptic Gospels. The Gospel of John contains only two parables: the Good Shepherd in John 10 and the Vine and the Branches in John 15.

## Jewish Roots of Jesus' Parables

When we speak of the Gospel parables, we must remind ourselves that we are not speaking of some kind of teaching device that Jesus used in a vacuum. The language of Jesus' parables comes to him from his Jewish heritage. Well after the life and times of Jesus of Nazareth, we can see this style of teaching in the writings of the rabbis whose works comprise the Talmud (the ongoing rabbinic interpretation of the written and the oral Torah/Law). Jesus is but one part of the historical puzzle of the Jewish parable; yet, as we shall see, Jesus made some unique contributions to this time-honored way of rabbinic teaching.

The earliest biblical parable is Jotham's parable of the trees, told to the people of Shechem in Judges 9:8-15. Nathan, David's prophet, uses a parable in 2 Samuel 12 to expose David's infidelity. But the parable appears much more often in the writings that compose the prophetic literature of the Hebrew Bible. Isaiah, Jeremiah and Ezekiel all use it at certain points.

Isaiah 5:1-7 tells a parable about a vineyard to call the people of Judah to recognize their infidelity to God. The prophet Ezekiel uses the parable form at least three times. Ezekiel 16 tells the story of a woman, raised alone in the desert by God, who becomes a harlot. Ezekiel 17 offers the allegory of the eagle—a parable about Judah's failed attempt to make an alliance with Egypt, thus betraying Babylon. Ezekiel 23 narrates the parable of the two sisters, Oholah and Oholibah, to tell the story of the unfaithfulness of Israel and Judah before the Babylonian exile.

The Wisdom Tradition of the Hebrew Scriptures also

provides examples of parabolic literature: the teaching narratives of Job, Jonah and Tobit. These stories reveal a mystery about faith in God. The wisdom teachers summarized admirable and corrupt human behavior in riddles and aphorisms:

> Whose offspring are worthy of honor?
>   Human offspring.
> Whose offspring are worthy of honor?
>   Those who fear the Lord.
> Whose offspring are unworthy of honor?
>   Human offspring.
> Whose offspring are unworthy of honor?
>   Those who break the commandments (Sirach 10:19).

The parable or riddle was a versatile tool in the hands of these skilled wisdom teachers. As a literary form, it was an important influence on Jesus. His short parables on salt and light, as well as those about lost sheep or coins or about leaven in the dough, suggest a tendency to teach with the parable or riddle.

If we are to understand the parable as a typical Jewish mode of teaching, we should look at the parables of the rabbis in the Talmud, a two-volume work. The first volume, the Palestinian Talmud, was finished in the fifth century C.E. The other volume, the Babylonian Talmud, was written in the mid-sixth century C.E. The Talmud is a commentary on the *Mishnah*, a collection of 63 tractates or treatises on Moses' Law compiled under one Rabbi Judah the Prince around 200 C.E. Present-day Judaism considers the Talmud the authoritative commentary on Jewish law.

The parables told in the Talmud have a very definite fourfold structure: motivation, followed by a key insight, the parable and the interpretation. Since the rabbinic parables were of a homiletic nature, they are full of colorful characters and images. One of the most frequently occurring characters is the king, who usually stands for God. Four categories of king parables told by the rabbis bear mentioning here, as they have obvious parallels in Jesus' parables: (1) the king as the ruler of all humankind; (2) the king as a father and Israel as his sons and daughters; (3) the king as a husband and Israel as his wife; (4) the king and his subjects, of whom Israel is his favorite.

Why did the rabbis—both Jesus' contemporaries and those long after him—tell parables? The immediate answer is to interpret the Torah (the first five books of the Hebrew Scriptures). The primary duty of the rabbi was to teach, so he had to find ways of making difficult scriptural verses speak to his audience. By telling stories, the rabbis could make abstract theological concepts accessible to the people before them. Another reason was to explain the relation between God and Israel; a third was ethical exhortation (the parables frequently deal with the consequences of improper behavior). Lastly, the Talmud parables touch on salvation history. By way of parable, the rabbis could explain and interpret God's past acts—as Jesus did.

## Jesus' Use of Parables

In Jesus, we meet a master in the art of telling parables. Jesus makes inventive use of his chosen form. Like Jotham and Nathan of old, Jesus uses the parable to challenge his listeners. Look at the parable of the Good Samaritan in Luke 10, or the Wicked Tenants in Matthew 21:33-41 (Isaiah 5:1-7, the story of the vineyard, is probably its source). Proverbs 9:1-5 speaks of Wisdom as a woman preparing a banquet, while in Luke 14:17-24, Jesus tells the parable of the great dinner to which many are invited. Jesus used images from nature—fig trees, sheep, farmers sowing seed. His characters are drawn from daily life—widows, tax collectors, soldiers and dishonest servants. The imagery, characters and situations Jesus drew from the Hebrew Scriptures.

Many of Jesus' parables appear to step right out of the Wisdom Literature tradition of Israel. The parables of salt and light from Matthew 5:13-16 are the kind of literary form we find in the Book of Proverbs or the writings of Sirach. Jesus' use of the short wisdom riddle is probably the basis for such parables as the Pearl of Great Price and the Buried Treasure

(Matthew 13:44-46), the parables of the Mustard Seed and the Yeast (Matthew 13:31-33). The unresponsive children in Matthew 11:16-17 and Luke 7:31-32 also echo the Wisdom Tradition.

It is fair to say that Jesus saw himself as God's last messenger before the final establishment of the Kingdom. He looked for a new order, created by the mighty acts of God. That said, it is not surprising that Jewish eschatological hopes—hopes about the final action of God—were a part of Jesus' teaching. The three parables of Matthew 25 (the Ten Bridesmaids, the Talents and the Separation of Sheep From Goats) reveal a Jesus who saw certain and decisive final judgment. The two parables from Mark 13:28-37 (the Fig Tree and the Vigilant Servants) remind us that Jesus' eschatological teaching was part of the tradition.

Did Jesus rely on the Hebrew Scriptures for the material of his parables? It is not possible to say with absolute certainty what Jesus knew or did not know about them. But we can say that his teachings bear such similarity to their style that it is hard to claim another background. The imagery he used, the style of his teaching and the presence of Jewish eschatological hopes all point to a foundation in the Hebrew Bible.

Both Jesus' parables and the parables told by the rabbis are drawn from daily life that common, unsophisticated folk would have felt at home with and understood: a woman kneading yeast into flour, a dispute between sons and a father, a man who has fallen in with robbers, lost sheep. Wedding banquets, people on journeys, kings, animals, farming—these are the images both Jesus and the rabbis chose. Is it possible to say Jesus was a trained rabbi because of these similarities? I do not think we have evidence to answer the question definitively, but considering Jesus' formative years, the answer is probably no.

Jesus' parables also differ from those of the rabbis. His are often more nuanced and developed in plot and character. The rabbis generally told parables to illustrate the meaning of a particular biblical text. Jesus made more creative use of his parables. They were often open-ended, allowing for more than one interpretation by his hearers. In the retelling, we can understand Jesus' parables on many different levels of meaning. For example, it is possible to read the parable of the Talents (Matthew 25:14-30) as a story about final judgment, yet it also could be about the right use of one's earthly goods.

What occasions, what life situations, prompted Jesus to tell a parable? Historically speaking, this is not an easy question to answer, since we only get to read Jesus' parables in the contexts the various evangelists chose for them. Yet it is possible to delineate two settings for Jesus' parables. One is Jesus preaching to a crowd (especially the kingdom parables). A second setting for parable is in Jesus' debates with the Pharisees and Sadducees, for example, the question about the debtors raised at Simon the Pharisee's house (Luke see 8:36-50), or in the story of the Wicked Tenants (Matthew 21:33-41).

The simplest of parables is the proverb. Jesus often used such short sayings of comparison that draw from ordinary experience to illustrate how life should be lived. Matthew's Sermon on the Mount provides an example of Jesus' use of proverbs, "You are the light of the world. A city built on a hill cannot be hid" (Matthew 5:14).

## Parables That Cause Us to Reflect About Ourselves

Jesus also narrated familiar experiences to reflect the deeper spiritual values of the Kingdom of God. An example is the parable of the Good Samaritan (see Luke 10:25-37). Jesus takes the experience of a fellow human being in need and shows that help knows no boundaries.

To understand this parable properly it is necessary to examine its context. A lawyer comes to Jesus with a question. Luke tells us that the lawyer intends to "test Jesus." According to Jesus, the law answers his question, "What must I do to inherit eternal life?" The lawyer proves his knowledge of the law, citing two central passages from the law concerning love of God and neighbor (Deuteronomy 6:4-5; Leviticus 19:18). Jesus affirms the lawyer's response, telling him to observe those commandments and he will have eternal life, thus answering the lawyer's question.

At first sight, this discussion between Jesus and the lawyer might seem unrelated to the parable that follows. The lawyer is not satisfied with the answer. Leviticus 19:18, which he has cited concerning love of neighbor, implies that "neighbor" means only one's fellow Jews. The lawyer wants Jesus to assure that this interpretation of the law is correct. Therefore he poses another question, "Who is my neighbor?" Jesus answers, telling the parable of the Good Samaritan.

A man who has fallen among robbers is near death. Two who are traveling on the same road, a priest and a Levite, avoid him. Their action is simply strict observance of the law about touching corpses. This man looks dead, therefore, they presume, he is. If they touch a corpse, they will become ritually unclean and cannot perform their duties in the templo. It is better to continue walking and not get involved.

Another traveler on the road sees the wounded man, cares for him, binds his wounds and gives him food. Then he brings him to an inn, and pays for his care until he can continue the journey. The parable contrasts the priest and the Levite with the man who helped. The contrast becomes more pointed since Jesus identifies the helper as a Samaritan.

Throughout the history of Israel, Jews and Samaritans regarded each other as enemies, so a Samaritan stopping to help a Jew is astonishing. When Jesus asks the lawyer who was "neighbor" to the man in need, we can be sure that the lawyer nearly choked on the answer. He never says, "the Samaritan," only "the one who showed mercy to him." The conclusion to the parable forces the lawyer to reflect on whom *he* considers "neighbor." In the parable's context, the answer to the lawyer's question concerning eternal life demands that he be neighbor to all those who are in need, no matter who they are. The parable demands that we evaluate our attitudes and behaviors toward all our neighbors. It challenges us to widen our horizons beyond racism or sexism.

## Parables That Help Us Understand Something About God

Parables can also give us a better idea of what God is really like. They provide a window through which we can glimpse the reality of God (God is like the Good Shepherd who lays down his life for his flock). Possibly the best example of this type of parable would be the Prodigal Son (Luke 15:11-32).

In truth, the Prodigal Son is probably the most vivid story Jesus tells in the Gospels. It is the third of three parables about the lost and found—the lost sheep, the lost coin, the lost son. The three parables answer a comment from the Pharisees and scribes concerning Jesus' presence with tax collectors and sinners. As with the parable of the Good Samaritan, the context is the prime indicator for how we should interpret the story.

It consists of four scenes. The first scene introduces the major characters, a father and his two sons, the younger of whom requests his portion of his father's property. Such a request implies a wish that the father die, since inheritances were meted out only after the death of the father. The father must be devastated. Yet he complies with his son's request, giving him his just portion. (Jewish law provided that an estate be divided among the sons, with the eldest receiving a double portion. In this case, the elder son would receive two-thirds while the younger would receive one-third.)

In the second scene, the younger son is in a distant land. After recklessly squandering his inheritance, he is reduced to feeding swine. Coming to his senses, he decides to return home. Thinking that he will no longer be welcomed as a son, he resolves to ask for a job as a hired hand. All the way home, he rehearses his speech to his father.

The third scene is his arrival home. His father greets him joyfully, kissing him, arraying him in a bright robe, giving him a ring and offering sandals for his feet. To the son's shock and surprise, the father treats him like a son. The servants are ordered to kill and cook a fatted calf, and the feast begins.

In the final scene, the older son is jealous. He feels cheated. He has faithfully and constantly served his father and his brother has not, but his father has never provided a party for him. If we look at the father's words to his older son and recall the question that introduced the parable (Why does Jesus eat with sinners?), the message is clear. Jesus, like the father, showers his love on whomever he wishes. The joy the father shows at the return of his lost son does not in any way detract from his love for his older son. The problem is that the older son is blinded to that love because of his own self-image: He views himself as a hired hand and has never allowed himself to experience his father's love. At the end, he remains unwilling to accept the fact of his father's love.

The Pharisees feel they have a corner on the father's love; they are unwilling to admit that the Father (God) can accept tax collectors and sinners. Like the older son in the parable, they are unable to experience a wider understanding of God's parental love. The parable also challenges the modern reader to consider his or her own God concept and the need for widening and revamping it.

## The Parables in the Gospel of Mark

In the Synoptic Gospels, Luke includes the most parables, followed by Matthew, with Mark having the fewest. Space does not allow an analysis here of all the Gospel parables. We will limit our comments to the Gospel of Mark, since it is the first written Gospel and the shortest, thus more manageable than either Matthew or Luke.

Mark's Gospel contains many small discourses. One of those, where Jesus taught in parables (Mark 3:23-30), sets the stage for the rest of his teachings in the Gospel.

As a teacher, Jesus must have spoken directly as well in stories and sayings. But the Gospels do not present these conversations or discourses word-for-word. The Gospels were written after the Resurrection with the intention of responding to new issues and problems in the Christian communities.

The parables are also literary devices. The evangelists who wrote the Gospels composed the "literary discourses" in the

73

Gospels. Parables are key elements in those discourses.

There is a difference, then, between a discourse, which marked an *historical* moment, and a *literary* discourse, which refers to the same moment in literature, in this case the Gospel of Mark. Historically, a discourse was delivered in one place, at one time, and for one particular audience. *Literarily*, however, an author could rise above the historical context. A discourse could start in one place and at a particular time and then, with little or no transition, jump to another place and time, freeing it to speak with a new voice for a new people confronting challenges of their own. This situation is the case with the parable of the Sower (Mark 4:1-34).

The beginning of the discourse is simple. According to the introduction Jesus spoke to a large crowd by the sea, and he spoke to them in parables (Mark 4:1-2).

The discourse then presents one, and only one, of the many parables Jesus told the crowd, that of the Sower (Mark 4:3-9). At this point, the audience changes. With the stroke of a pen, the crowd disappears and Jesus is "alone with those who were around him along with the twelve" (Mark 4:10a). His message to them unfolds in three parts: (1) He explains why he spoke in parables (Mark 4:10-12); (2) he interprets for them the parable of the Sower (Mark 4:13-20); (3) he concludes by speaking further about parables and their purpose (Mark 4:21-25).

The discourse then returns to its original audience, and Jesus presents two further parables to the crowd, both of them concerning the Kingdom of God (Mark 4:26-32). The discourse ends with a conclusion reaffirming the distinction between Jesus' teaching to the crowds, which was done with many such parables, and his teaching to his own disciples, which included private explanations (Mark 4:33-34).

In Mark's literary discourse, Jesus has three distinct audiences: the crowd (4:1), those who were around him with the Twelve (4:10) and his own disciples (4:34). In the narrator's introduction (Mark 4:1-2), and conclusion (Mark 4:33-34), as well as in Jesus' message to his own disciples (Mark 4:10-12), the Gospel says that Jesus addressed the two audiences differently. He spoke *publicly* to the crowds in parables but he explained the parables in *private* only to his disciples, that is, those who were around him with the Twelve.

With these distinctions, we can show how Mark has built a bridge between the historical time of Jesus, when the parables were quite clear, and the evangelist's own time, when they required some explanation. Once explained, the parables again became clear, but only for those who gather around Jesus with the Twelve.

The discourse includes yet another important distinction between those who were "around Jesus" (Mark 4:10; see also Mark 3:32) with the Twelve, and those who were outside (Mark 4:11; see also 3:32). For those outside, not only do the parables remain obscure, but also no explanation will suffice to clarify them (Mark 4:12). To understand the parables, you have to be an intimate follower of Jesus and associated with the Twelve in the new Israel. In a sense, you have to be a part of the inner group.

### Jesus' Teaching by the Sea (Mark 4:1)

Such a large crowd gathered to hear Jesus teach by the sea that he sat in a boat on the water while the crowd stayed on the land. Such is the physical setting of Jesus' great discourse in parables.

The first time Jesus went by the sea, he called Simon and Andrew, James and John to follow him (Mark 1:16-20). The second time he went by the sea he taught the crowd and called Levi to follow him (Mark 2:13-17). The second event recalled the first. Not only did Jesus go to the sea; he went *again* by the sea (see Mark 2:13).

Such is also the case this third time Jesus goes to teach by the sea: He went *again*. Each time Jesus returns to the sea, the Gospel of Mark recalls the previous time and invites us to think of those events as a group. They are the events that took place by the sea, just as there are the events in Mark that took place on the mountain and in the desert.

The setting of the parable discourse also recalls the

introductory summary for this whole section of the Gospel (3:7-12). The previous summary situated Jesus' proclamation of the Gospel in Galilee (1:14-15). In this second major summary, Jesus withdraws toward the sea. The summary also describes the crowd that gathered for this teaching as coming from all of Galilee and Judea, Jerusalem and even from the neighboring Gentile lands. Jesus asks to have a boat ready for him lest he be crushed by the crowd (3:9). This seems strange, since Jesus does not immediately use the boat, but goes up to the mountain (Mark 3:13) and then home (Mark 3:20).

The naming of the Twelve, which took place on the mountain (3:13-19), and the subsequent teaching at home (3:20-35) very important theologically and literarily, but they interrupt Jesus' teaching by the sea. The Gospel consequently establishes a fresh link between 3:7-12 and 4:1-34. The boat had already been prepared (3:9), and now as the huge crowd gathers, Jesus has only to get into it.

Jesus wonderfully positions everyone for the discourse. The setting is a natural amphitheater because the water that separated Jesus and the crowd provides natural amplification.

The crowd was on land but on the very edge of chaos, symbolized by the sea. Jesus was in the boat in the teacher's position—seated—dominating the chaos. After the discourse, Jesus will remain in the boat and cross the sea with his disciples. His rebuke will quiet the violent storm— symbolizing chaos—and bring on a great calm (Mark 4:35-41). Still later, Jesus will even walk out to his disciples on the stormy sea (Mark 6:45-52). For the discourse in parables, he merely sits on the sea in the boat, but the story of Jesus and the new Israel has barely begun. Yet, when Jesus the storyteller spins a yarn, chaos does not reign supreme; he conquers it.

### Teaching in Parables (Mark 4:2)

This is the second time in the Gospel that Jesus is said to have taught in parables (see Mark 3:23). "Teaching in parables" is different from saying that Jesus "told" parables. It describes the method of teaching and implies that this method was chosen for a special purpose.

"Teaching in parables" usually implies that several parables were presented. The Gospel states that Jesus spoke with many parables on this occasion (Mark 4:33). At this point, however, only one of those parables is retold: the Sower and the Seed.

### The Parable of the Sower and the Seed (Mark 4:3-9)

To get the crowd's full attention, Jesus gives the parable a one-word preface, "Listen!" as he launches into "A sower went out to sow" (Mark 4:3).

The parable could easily have focused on the sower and the act of sowing, but it does not. These merely provide a literary setting for the seed, the kinds of ground on which it fell and what subsequently happened to it (Mark 4:4-8). The parable focuses mostly on the soil: the path, the rocky ground, the thorns and the rich soil. The seed is the same in each case. What differs is the ground. What happens to the seed depends entirely on where it falls.

It is easy to misinterpret a parable. In this example, the temptation is to associate the different kinds of ground with distinct categories of people. Instead, we should interpret the parable as a challenge to each of Jesus' listeners, inviting all to reflect on how he or she is responding to Jesus' ministry, measuring their response against the ideal of the rich soil that yields an abundant harvest.

A brief epilogue, "Let anyone with ears to hear listen!" (4:9), recalls the one-word preface, "Listen!" (4:3). The preface and the epilogue, with their emphasis on hearing, make the parable a good introduction for the remainder of the discourse, which deals with the problem of truly hearing and understanding the parables.

### The Purpose of the Parables According to Mark (Mark 4:10-12)

After the parable and Jesus' challenge to hear (Mark 4:3-9), the crowd disappears. Jesus and the Twelve are alone. They question him about the parables. Jesus explains why they were able to understand while those outside were not.

Those with the Twelve have been granted the mystery of the Kingdom of God (see 1:14-15). As part of the new Israel, open to Jew and Gentile, they have the experience that allows them to understand. What was hidden in the past, and even now is hidden from others, God has revealed to them.

Those who remain outside have not received the mystery of the Kingdom of God, whereby all human beings are called to participate in the new Israel. For them, Jesus' teaching in parables remains opaque. They lack the experience of faith and commitment that would allow them to understand. As a result, the intrinsic purpose of the parables ends up being exactly the opposite of what Jesus meant it to be. What should bring perception and understanding does not.

The Gospel of Mark says that even what they see and hear will lose its former meaning lest they be converted and forgiven. An era has ended! The conversion associated with the old era, even that preached by John the Baptizer (1:4), no longer suffices. A new era has begun, that of the new Israel, ushering in the universal Kingdom of God. For those who do not enter the new era, the religious circuits that fed the old are short-circuited. For those who have capitulated to Satan and blasphemed against the Holy Spirit there can be no forgiveness (Mark 3:29).

**The Sower and the Seed: Jesus Offers a New Interpretation (Mark 4:13-20)**

After explaining the purpose of the parables (4:10-12; see 4:2), Jesus interprets the one parable presented while he was addressing the whole crowd (4:3-9). If the disciples do not understand this parable, how can they understand any of the others (4:13)? The parable of the Sower and the Seed was not selected at random. This parable provides the key for understanding all the others.

In his interpretation, Jesus identifies the seed as the word. He then shows what happened to the word that fell on the path, on rocky ground, among thorns and on rich soil. In the first telling of the parable (4:3-9), emphasis lay on the seed and what happened to it.

In the interpretation, Jesus shifts the emphasis from the seed to the various kinds of ground. He mentions again the rich ground, the climax of the first telling, and the ideal against which one can measure oneself, but without additional development. The other kinds of ground and what happened to seeds that fell on them receives a new and imaginative treatment.

The development and interpretation of this parable are quite similar to some parabolic and allegorical teachings found in the *Mishna* in the tractate called *The Fathers*. In that format, the explanation takes the following structure:

There are three types of disciples in whom the word is sown, and there is a fourth kind:

—the path from whom the word is immediately snatched away by Satan, the tempter; they hardly even hear the word;

—the rocky ground, in whom the word is joyfully received but has no roots; they hear the word but fall away when tribulation or persecution comes because of the word;

—the thorns in whom the word is choked by worldly anxiety, the lure of riches, or craving for other things; they hear the word but it bears no fruit;

—the rich soil; they not only hear the word, but accept it and it bears fruit thirty and sixty and one-hundred fold.

The first telling of the parable held up an ideal. The second interpretation aimed at moral formation. In presenting it, Mark may have meant to evoke the disciples' baptismal commitment. This interpretation is suggested by two themes, the sowing of the word and the bearing of fruit.

As he evoked the baptismal commitment, Mark also held it up to the challenges faced by the early Christians, including his readers, who experienced tribulation, persecution, worldly anxiety, the lure of riches and other cravings.

**Parables for the Disciples (Mark 4:21-25)**

Jesus now turns to the disciples' mission regarding the mystery of the Kingdom of God. For this, Mark presents two short parables, the Lamp and the Measure, along with their interpretation (Mark 4:21-25).

The lamp is not placed under a basket or under a bed, but on a lamp stand. Why? Because nothing is hidden or secret (Mark 4:21-22). Jesus means for parables to enlighten, which is why he must make their meaning plain for those who have been granted the mystery of the Kingdom of God (see 4:11-12).

The little parable of the lamp and its interpretation have a brief epilogue, very similar to the one that followed the parable of the Sower and the Seed (4:9): "Let anyone with ears to hear listen!" (4:23). This time, however, Jesus addresses it not to the crowd, but to the disciples, who should not take their hearing for granted—as Jesus has just shown in his interpretation of the Sower and the Seed (4:13-20). Not everyone who receives the word receives it the same way, and not everyone perseveres.

The theme of hearing also introduces the second little parable, the Measure: "Pay attention to what you hear; the measure you give will be the measure you get, and still more will be given you. For to those who have, more will be given; and from those who have nothing, even what they have will be taken away" (4:24-25).

One who has will be given more; one who has been granted the mystery of the Kingdom (see 4:11a) will receive new understanding because of it (4:13-20). One who has not will lose even what he or she has (4:25b). Those who have not been granted the mystery of the Kingdom, who are not with the Twelve and who remain outsiders, will lose even that sight and hearing they had once enjoyed. Everything will become opaque to them (4:12b). Mark uses the words of Isaiah 6:9-10 to make his point and also directs them as a warning to those who receive the word on a path, on rocky ground or among thorns.

## Parables of the Kingdom of God (Mark 4:26-32)

Jesus' special teaching for the disciples is over. The crowd reappears on the seashore and Jesus is again teaching from the boat on the sea (see 4:33-34). The discourse concludes with two parables further developing the image of the seed.

The first draws attention to the seed's growth, which goes on mysteriously, inexorably and independently of human effort once it is sown. The seed grows and matures all the way to the harvest (4:26-29). The parable enables Jesus' listeners to see how the Kingdom continues to grow without fanfare.

It also evokes Jesus' own life and mission. Jesus has planted the word, which then grows and develops in the course of history. When the world grows to maturity in the Kingdom of God, Jesus will return for the harvest (see 13:24-37).

The discourse concludes with the parable of the Mustard Seed, the tiniest of all seeds. This time, the parable does not tell of the mystery of growth. It describes the way an extraordinary plant with great branches comes from practically nothing (Mark 4:30-32). So it is with God's Reign, which begins as a tiny seed which will eventually grow into God's universal dominion.

Mark means for parables to reassure his community about the value of their commitment to follow Christ in the new Israel. Once planted, the seed continues to grow from a modest beginning to full maturity.

The remaining two parables in the Gospel of Mark are interesting. The first, the parable of the vineyard and the wicked tenants (Mark 12:1-11) comments on the hostility toward Jesus. It then places the harsh treatment given to Jesus in the tradition of God's earlier messengers, the prophets. There are some obvious identifications in the parable as it stands: The vineyard is Israel, the owner is God, the tenant farmers are Israel's leaders, the beloved son is Jesus. Most likely, the servants are the prophets; and the "others" are the Gentiles. The context of the parable is the relationship between Jesus and his opponents and, by implication, the

Marcan Church and its opponents.

The final parable, the Fig Tree (Mark 13:28-29), makes use of nature. The fig tree's natural process of growth in spring and summer is compared with the sequence of events leading up to the coming of the Son of Man. The implication is that when you see these events happening, you will know that the Son of Man will come soon to usher in the final Reign of God.

## Conclusion

It seems from reading the Gospels that even Jesus' inner circle had trouble interpreting some parables. So we should not be shocked if we have trouble as well. Jesus' intimates often asked for an explanation—and they received one. Parables need explanation.

As a modern reader of the Gospels, you may often find it helpful to place yourself within the scene of the parable or to identify with one or more of the characters. Then you can recast the story in a contemporary setting, retaining the characters, the original elements of the plot and the moral of the story. A recasting of the parable of the Prodigal Child (Luke 15:11-32) or the Good Samaritan (Luke 10:29-37) can provide a deeper and richer understanding and an application to your own faith life.

### For Discussion

1) *What are the Jewish roots of the parable and why did Jesus teach in parables?*

2) *Why do you have to be an intimate follower of Jesus to understand his parables? Does this make sense to you? Why or why not?*

3) *Is Jesus the only one who can interpret the parable of your life?*

4) *How are you challenged by the parables of Jesus to examine and reflect on your own life?*

## For Further Reading

Boucher, Madeline I. *The Parables*. Wilmington, Del.: Michael Glazier, 1981.

Crossan, John Dominic. *In Parables: The Challenge of the Historical Jesus*. San Francisco: Harper & Row, 1973.

Dodd, Charles H. *The Parables of the Kingdom*. New York: Charles Scribner Sons, 1961.

Donahue, John R. *The Gospel in Parable: Metaphor, Narrative and Theology in the Synoptic Gospels*. Philadelphia: Fortress Press, 1988.

Drury, John. *The Parables in the Gospels: History & Allegory*. New York: Crossroad, 1985.

Funk, Robert W., Bernard Brandon Scott and James R. Butts. *The Parables of Jesus*. Sonoma, Calif.: Polebridge, 1988.

Jeremias, Joachim. *The Parables of Jesus*. London: SCM, 1962.

McKenna, Megan. *Parables, the Arrows of God*. Maryknoll, N.Y.: Orbis Books, 1994.

Perkins, Pheme. *Hearing the Parables of Jesus*. Mahwah, N.J.: Paulist Press, 1984.

Scott, Bernard Brandon. *Hear Then the Parable: A Commentary on the Parables of Jesus*. Minneapolis: Fortress Press, 1989.

Thoma, Clemens and Michael Wyschogrod, eds. *Parable and Story in Judaism and Christianity*. New York: Paulist Press, 1989.

CHAPTER SIX

# At the Table of the Lord

We all love a good meal. A meal is more than just food, it includes preparation, cooking, dining and conversation. Dining with friends is a sign of kinship. In the Hebrew Scriptures, the image most often used for heaven is that of a banquet. The prophet Isaiah writes:

> On this mountain the LORD of hosts will make for all peoples
> a feast of rich food, a feast of well-aged wines,
> of rich food filled with marrow, of well-aged wines strained clear (25:6).

The best meals are a time of rejoicing and celebration, a time of sustenance laced with fellowship and community. They are times when the burdens of the world seem lost to us, when we are drawn up into a different and better reality.

In the Ancient Near Eastern world, meals often served as acts of hospitality, as when Abraham welcomed the guests whom God had sent to inform him and Sarah that they were going to have a child (see Genesis 18:1-8). For the ancients, meals were rituals, for they provided not only physical sustenance, but food for the life of the spirit. Meals were where one encountered both fellow human beings and God.

Meals were also times of reconciliation, where alienated parties sat and forgave one another. To be disloyal, to take advantage of someone's table hospitality, to betray one's host were considered the most despicable of sins. The psalmist bemoans the very thought of betrayal from a trusted companion:

> Even my bosom friend in whom I trusted,

who ate of my bread, has lifted the heel against me (Psalm 41:9).

A meal played an important role in the sealing of the covenant between God and the people. In Exodus 24:1-11, the covenant at Sinai is sealed both in blood and in a meal eaten before God. Moses and the leaders "...beheld God, and they ate and drank" (Exodus 24:11b). This festive meal celebrated the covenant relationship and fellowship the people had with one another and with God.

Possibly the best remembered meal in the Hebrew Scriptures is Passover, described in Exodus 12. The most significant of the Jewish festivals, the feast commemorates God's angel passing over the Hebrew houses marked in blood and sparing their children from death. It is a festival seen as a celebration of freedom from slavery as the Hebrews passed over the Red Sea to a new life with their God. Jews still celebrate Passover today. As we will see later, the Passover meal forms the backdrop for the Last Supper in the Christian Scriptures.

Throughout the Gospels, Jesus shares meals with a variety of people. For Jesus, a meal was more than just a way to fill his stomach. A meal was a way to teach about the love God was extending to all men and women, especially those most in need of God's message. Jesus' meals with the poor, sinners and outcasts were signs of solidarity with the despised and rejected. These meals were signs of the future heavenly banquet. They were images of what it would be like to dine in the Kingdom of God.

From scattered clues throughout the Gospels we can glimpse something of the etiquette that prevailed at banquets given by the well-to-do at the time the Gospel writers formulated the Christian Scriptures. Etiquette prescribed, for example, appropriate clothes for guests (Matthew 22:11-12) and the host's obligation to greet the guests with a kiss and provide for the washing of their feet (Luke 7:44-45). In the Palestine of Jesus' day, it was apparently customary to issue two invitations to a banquet—the first one some days ahead of time, and the second when the meal was ready (Luke 14:16-17). Once they arrived, the guests were seated according to age or rank (see Luke 14:7-10).

In describing meals that Jesus participated in, the Gospels say that he reclined at table. This expression suggests the Greco-Roman custom of reclining at formal meals had become widespread. On couches placed around a large table (or possibly three tables placed to form an open-ended rectangle), guests and host reclined on the left elbow and ate with the right hand, their feet extending off the back of the couch. Usually, three persons reclined on one couch. This posture at table enabled the sinful woman to stand behind Jesus while anointing his feet (Luke 7:36-38). It also explains how Jesus could wash the disciples' feet as they ate (John 13), and how the beloved disciple could recline on Jesus' breast (John 13:23).

In Jesus' day, the blessing of the food at the beginning of a meal had become standard practice in Judaism; a prayer of thanksgiving over a cup of wine concluded the meal. The observant Pharisees, in addition, insisted on the ritual washing of hands. Although Jesus blessed the food before eating, he and his disciples did not adopt the practice of hand-washing (Mark 7:1-5; Luke 11:37-37).

Jesus' table fellowship with his followers was an important feature of his public ministry and, according to the Gospels, his eating with "tax collectors and sinners" drew criticism from his detractors. The accusation that he was a "glutton and drunkard" (Matthew 11:18-19; Luke 7:33-34) suggests that, unlike John the Baptizer, Jesus took pleasure in eating and drinking. He intended his table fellowship to symbolize for his companions the blessing of joyous fellowship in God's presence that would characterize the new age. In the Lord's Prayer, according to one understanding, Jesus taught his disciples to pray "...give us this day our daily bread" as a plea for God to allow a foretaste of future blessedness amid the afflictions and failures of the present age.

Several times in the Gospels, a meal is the setting for important teachings of Jesus. Some of Jesus' parables have to do with a feast or feasting.

Meals are also the context for revelation about Jesus. Some of the risen Jesus' appearances to his disciples occur in the context of a meal. It was only when Jesus blessed and broke the bread that Cleopas and his companion recognized him (Luke 24:30-31). In John 21, the Risen One gives his disciples bread and fish to eat beside the Sea of Tiberias (21:9-13; see Luke 24:41-43).

Meals are an important part of Jesus' proclamation of the Kingdom of God. This observation is especially true in the Gospel of Luke, where ten meal narratives appear. During many meals, Jesus both manifests his mission and teachings, as well as his power and glory. Often during his ministry, friends, officials and poor people invited Jesus to share a meal.

## Jesus' Meals in the Gospels

At the wedding in Cana (John 2:1-11), to which Jesus was invited along with his mother and disciples, he appears as one guest among others. When the wine runs out, his mother solicits Jesus' help. He immediately changes water into wine, an excellent vintage that in an unexpected way rejoices the hearts of guests and host alike. In the vocabulary of John's Gospel, wine given to human beings within the context of a wedding feast is a glimpse of the final Messianic banquet all will enjoy with Jesus.

The meal Jesus eats in the home of Matthew (Matthew 9:10-13) has another meaning. The newly recruited disciple, Matthew, wishes to throw a party to celebrate his new vocation by inviting Jesus to table with his friends—who are, like him, tax collectors and people of ill repute. By accepting Matthew's invitation, Jesus transforms the meaning of the occasion. Instead of being received, it is he who receives these sinners and sick people he has come to seek. These people, whom society ostracized and the religious establishment excommunicated, are welcomed by Jesus to the community (or communion) of his disciples.

The Gospel of Luke (5:29) provides a similar account of this banquet. Having come as a guest, Jesus reverses the roles and becomes the host who invites and gathers the sick, the poor and the marginalized. Jesus then transforms this meal into a locus of healing and welcome. Jesus' bold gesture of welcoming or accepting invitations to table fellowship with outcasts and sinners was a shocking yet compelling expression of God's inclusion of those outside the Jewish community in the saving experience of the Kingdom.

Once, when Simon the Pharisee invites Jesus to eat at his home (Luke 7:36-50), a woman reputed to be a sinner finds her way into the dining room, weeps her repentance and receives pardon for her sins. Jesus becomes accessible to a woman, and this meal is the place of the forgiveness of sins. In a more subtle way, this meal also reveals the identity of each of those who dine with Jesus: Simon, who has not performed his duties as host as well as he thinks (7:44-47); the reputed sinner, who has given proof of great love (7:39, 47-48); and Jesus himself (7:39, 40). It seems impossible for people to dine with Jesus without their masks falling from their faces.

Invited to the home of Martha and Mary, his friends, Jesus proposes another teaching in giving these two women to understand that he comes to give rather than to receive (Luke 10:38-42). If anyone presumes to welcome him, let that person not become preoccupied with preparing a great dinner, but instead leave herself time to listen. Jesus' table talk is the food of the meal, which Mary recognizes more than her sister, Martha.

The meal at the home of a Pharisee during which Jesus heals a man suffering from dropsy on a sabbath (Luke 14:1-6) provides not only a new interpretation of sabbath, but also an occasion to affirm the relationship between meal and healing. Jesus suggests that people should not sit and take nourishment without concerning themselves for those who live in difficult conditions. Thus Jesus makes the human meal the means of fulfilling all hunger, of restoring life afflicted with infirmity.

The meal to which Jesus is invited at Bethany a few days before his Passion takes place at the home of Simon the Leper in Matthew 26:6-13 and Mark 14:3-9, but at the home of Mary and Martha in John 12:1-11. At the house of Simon the Leper, an unnamed woman anoints Jesus and then his angry disciples rebuke her. Jesus immediately interprets her actions as appropriate, preparing him for burial, and the disciples' as inappropriate, wanting to dismiss the woman's action as an expensive waste of costly ointment. The point is that when people dine with Jesus, Jesus decides the appropriateness of their behavior at table, not the other guests or the host.

In John's account, the story is different. While it still takes place at Bethany, the guests include Martha, who served the meal, Lazarus, who had been raised from the dead by Jesus, and Mary, who anoints Jesus' feet with some expensive perfume. This time Judas protests, saying the costly ointment should have been sold and the money given to the poor, thus completely dismissing the meaning of Mary's actions. Jesus rebukes him, saying: "Leave her alone" (12:7), affirming her action as preparation for his burial.

Interestingly, in both stories Jesus, whom the Gospel writers understand to be God's anointed, is anointed not by the proper religious authority, the high priest, but by women and within the context of a meal. Just as the ointment penetrates Jesus' skin, reminding us that he is God's anointed (Messiah), the story penetrates ours. We do not decide what fellowship with Jesus entails; this he alone can do, and it is most often done at table, the place of nourishment.

Other meals important to Jesus' ministry include the healing of Peter's mother-in-law who, hardly back on her feet, begins to serve Jesus and his first disciples (Mark 1:29-31); the resurrection of the daughter of Jairus, whom Jesus recommends feeding (Mark 5:43); and the reception in the home of Zacchaeus, a sinner to whom Jesus brings salvation. Invited to table by a variety of people, Jesus manifests himself as the bringer of comfort, of healing, of life and of joy. Whatever the guests might have expected of the meal, they discover it is Jesus who gives it, but at a deeper level. For people who are hungry he becomes true nourishment, that which restores, renews, gives life. For people who are thirsty, he becomes a true drink. For people who are sinners he becomes the forgiver. We can say that at these meals Jesus communicates and celebrates the salvation that comes from God.

## Post-Resurrection Meals

Besides the meals Jesus partakes of during his public life, the Gospels also record meals with his disciples after the Resurrection. It is striking to note that in the brief time from the Resurrection to Jesus' Ascension, meals with his disciples play an integral role. The Gospels mention a variety of meals during which the risen Jesus manifests himself to disciples still hesitant in faith. On Easter evening, after a long walk and a lengthy explanation of the Scriptures, the disciples on the road to Emmaus recognize Jesus during the breaking of the bread (Luke 24:13-35). That same evening, he appears to the Eleven, "while they were at table," and reproaches them for their unbelief (Mark 16:14)—probably the same appearance as in Luke 24:36-43, in which, in order to overcome the apostles' disbelief, Jesus eats some grilled fish in their sight. Finally, on the shore of the Lake of Tiberias, Jesus again makes himself known to some of his apostles by inviting them to breakfast with bread and fish that he himself has grilled for them (John 21:9-14).

The primary purpose of these meals is to convince the disciples of the reality of the Lord's Resurrection. The Lucan account offers two convincing experiences: On the one hand, Jesus shows the apostles his hands and feet, that is, the traces of the crucifixion; on the other hand, he eats before them to convince them that he is alive. Luke offers both as a response to unbelief.

## Last Supper/Passover

Among the meals that Jesus ate with his disciples, the most important is obviously the one we call the Last Supper. To understand the meaning of this meal, we need to reflect on its rootedness in Passover.

In the first century C.E., when Jesus of Nazareth lived, Jews celebrated the Passover meal only in Jerusalem, because the entire animal (a lamb or kid) had to be slaughtered in the Temple. Passover was a pilgrimage festival because large crowds of men, women and children went to Jerusalem and the Temple to celebrate it. Luke 2:41-44 leads us to believe that Jesus and his family did this; when Mary and Joseph lost Jesus in the Temple, the family had gone to Jerusalem to celebrate Passover.

In Jerusalem the Passover crowds were so great that people could eat the sacrificial meal anywhere in the city, not just in the Temple precincts. Exodus 12 directs the group eating the meal to be large enough to consume the animal—ten to twenty people, most often an extended family. They gathered in rented rooms or sometimes in tents—anywhere a group could cook and eat a meal. They ate the meal after dark because the Jewish religious day begins with sundown and extends until sundown the next day. (Thus, Passover begins in the evening.) The group ate the foods prescribed in the Bible: the sacrificial animal, unleavened bread and bitter herbs. For the following seven days, they ate unleavened bread. Bitter herbs in small quantities served as a reminder of slavery in Egypt. Since wine, symbolic of joy, was the ordinary drink in Palestine, we can assume they consumed it as a matter of course.

We have no copy of the prescribed order of celebration for the Passover meal from the time of Jesus. Even the Gospel accounts of Jesus' last meal, which imply that it was a Passover meal, fail to give a complete account of what went on. Scholars conjecture—and I emphasize the word *conjecture*—that the Passover meal up to the destruction of the Jerusalem Temple by the Romans in 70 C.E., went as follows:

Like any festival meal, it began with a blessing over wine: "Blessed are you, Lord, our God, Creator of the fruit of the vine." This blessing was frequently followed or preceded by a prayer praising God for the special day being celebrated. Next they had hors d'oeuvres—vegetables such as lettuce and celery dipped in vinegar or some kind of sauce, possibly served with an initial cup of wine. The meal followed, initiated by a blessing said over the unleavened bread: "Blessed are you Lord, our God, ruler of the universe, who brings forth bread from the earth." The participants fulfilled the biblical commandments by eating the sacrificial animal, unleavened bread and bitter herbs. The meal proper concluded with a blessing over a cup of wine. (If Jesus' Last Supper with his disciples was a Passover meal, it is likely that these two blessings, the grace before the meal over the bread and the grace after the meal over the cup of wine, were the occasion for his declaration that the bread and wine are his body and blood.)

After the meal, the leader explained its meaning and retold the story of the first Passover. After the singing of the great Hallel, the psalms of praise (113-118), the festivities at the time of Jesus frequently ended with a final cup of wine.

Jesus and his followers took this Jewish ritual and transformed it into a new feast with analogous meaning. By it, God's Christian people are saved as God's Jewish people were saved before. Without this rich Jewish milieu, Jesus of Nazareth could not have explained his message and mission, nor could his early followers have understood him. Jesus celebrated the Passover and the writers of the Christian Scriptures understood (interpreted) him in faith as the Passover Lamb.

With this background in mind, we turn to the Christian Scriptures. Christians especially value the Jewish Passover festival because Jesus died and rose during its celebration. The Christian belief that Jesus' death atoned for humanity's sins and that his resurrection has given us new life grows out of Jewish belief. In the first Passover, narrated in Exodus 12, God saved the Hebrew people. The Passover ritual associates this original act of salvation with all the subsequent times God saves Israel.

Jesus died and rose around the time of Passover, but the Christian Scriptures do not clearly tell us whether Jesus' last meal with his followers was a Passover meal. Even if it was not a Passover Seder, the early Christian believers and the Gospel writers who recorded their tradition and beliefs linked the final hours of Jesus with the Passover celebration and used Passover symbolism and allusion to understand Jesus' actions. This linkage is natural because the earliest Christians were Jews who believed that Jesus was the Messiah appointed by God and sent to save God's people and initiate a time of justice and peace. These early believers were not yet a socially distinct group who called themselves "Christians." A generation or two after Jesus, during the writing of the Gospels (70-100 C.E.) Christians without a Jewish background still were familiar with Jewish traditions, including Passover, and expressed themselves in Jewish terms.

More importantly, Christians adapted the imagery of Exodus 12 and Leviticus 22:19-25 to explain the meaning of the Christ event. The four Gospels contain a variety of teachings about Passover. These teachings, including the Last Supper narratives, are theological reflections on the meaning of the passion, death and resurrection of Jesus.

### The Synoptic Accounts

The Gospel of Mark contains the following elements: the context for the Passover celebration (Mark 14:1-2); the preparations for the meal (Jesus sends someone into town to find the room in Mark 14:12-16); the description of the meal (Mark 14:22-25); and a conclusion: "When they had sung the hymn, they went out to the Mount of Olives" (Mark 14:26). Though Mark pictures Jesus' final meal with his disciples as a Passover meal (see Mark 14:12, 16), we are not certain that the final supper was a Passover. Jesus celebrates the Passover meal with his disciples in the evening because the Passover feast began at sundown and ran until sundown the next day. The Romans crucified him the next day, on Passover.

Matthew and Luke follow Mark on this. John's Gospel, however, says that the day on which Jesus was crucified was Preparation Day, the day the Passover lamb was sacrificed (John 19:14; see also 18:28). In John, then, Jesus' meal with his disciples was not the Passover meal, but an ordinary meal the evening before Passover.

The transformation of the Jewish Passover into the Christian Eucharist began with identifying Jesus' last meal with the Passover meal. Even if this identification is not historically verifiable, it was at least a theological identification. Mark's Gospel presents a problem because he does not say that a meal took place between the blessing of the bread and the blessing of the wine, whereas Luke and Paul both imply it did. Mark concludes his narrative with hymn-singing, which suggests the Hallel, psalms of praise that were the last prescribed prayer in the Passover ritual.

Matthew's Gospel, the most Jewish Gospel in the Christian Scriptures, provides a context (Matthew 26:2); the preparations (Matthew 26:17-19); a description of the meal (Matthew 26:26-29); and a conclusion (Matthew 26:30). To Mark's interpretation, Matthew adds a phrase to the blessing over the cup: "...for this is my blood of the covenant, *which is poured out for many for the forgiveness of sins*" (Matthew 26:28, emphasis added). In Matthew, the precise result of Jesus' death and the covenant with God is the forgiveness of sins. Just as the sacrifice in the Temple atoned for sins, and the Passover lamb saved the Israelites from death, Jesus' self-sacrifice, according to Matthew, saves believers from sin and brings about their forgiveness. Matthew links forgiveness to Jesus' death and to the celebration of the Lord's Supper, the memorial of his death.

Luke's outline is very similar outline to those of Mark and Matthew: the context (Luke 22:7), the preparations (Luke 22:8-13), the description of the meal (Luke 22:14-18 and 22:19-20), and the conclusion (Luke 22:39). When Jesus arranges to celebrate the Passover meal in Luke's Gospel, he tells Peter and John: "Go and prepare the Passover meal for us that we may eat it" (Luke 22:8). *For us* is not found in Matthew or

Mark. Jesus states his love for his disciples more explicitly in Luke's Gospel when he begins the meal by telling the apostles: "I have eagerly desired to eat this Passover with you before I suffer" (Luke 22:15).

Luke tells the story of Jesus' giving the disciples the bread and wine twice (Luke 22:15-18; 22:19-20). The first account stresses the link between this meal and the future Messianic banquet. The second, in which Jesus says "This is my body...this is my blood" is similar to the liturgical formula found in Paul's First Letter to the Corinthians and probably comes from the liturgy familiar to Luke and his community. In sum, the early Church, who composed the Gospels, in faith interpreted Jesus' last meal as a Passover Seder.

This theme of Passover is picked up in other parts of the Christian Scriptures: in 1 Corinthians 5 and 1 Peter 1:18-19; the Book of Revelation makes a theological identification between Jesus, the Lamb, and Passover (Revelation 5:6-14).

Paul sees Jesus as a type of Passover lamb: "For our paschal lamb, Christ, has been sacrificed" (1 Corinthians 5:7b). In 1 Corinthians 5:6-8 Paul theologizes on this meaning. Any observant Jew knows you have to purge the whole house of leaven before the feast of Passover. Paul says you now have to purge yourself of malice and develop a new moral behavior before you celebrate the feast of "Christ our Paschal Lamb."

In 1 Peter 1:18-19, the author states that the followers of Jesus are ransomed "...with the precious blood of Christ, like that of a lamb without defect or blemish." This notion is, of course, taken from Exodus, where the lamb used for the Passover celebration was to be without blemish or spot. This author is also theologizing out of his Jewish roots about the meaning of the Christ event. The preeminent lamb that saved Israel is, of course, the Passover lamb—in Egypt and in all subsequent celebrations. Both the Passover lamb (Exodus 12:5) and any lamb offered at the Temple (Leviticus 22:19-25) had to be perfect, without any ritual blemish. For the author of 1 Peter, Christ is this perfect offering.

The major symbol for Jesus in the Book of Revelation is the

Lamb: "Then I saw between the throne and the four living creatures and among the elders a Lamb standing as if it had been slaughtered..." (Revelation 5:6).

The Lamb who was slain is praised as one who is worthy "to receive power and wealth and wisdom and might / and honor and glory and blessing!" (Revelation 5:12). The Lamb who was slain saves. Revelation describes the saved in heaven as those: "...who have come out of the great ordeal; they have washed their robes and made them white in the blood of the Lamb" (7:14b). Just as the weakness of the Hebrews at Passover led to their ultimate success as a nation, so the Lamb's weakness, sacrifice and death have led to his exalted position with God in heaven.

These Christian Scriptures writers then are picking up these themes from their ancestral Jewish roots.

### Seder/Last Supper

As the Seder has a ritual of celebration, so does the Eucharist. The Passover Seder and the Christian Eucharist touch at four points:

1) Both celebrate an exodus, a delivery from bondage to freedom. The Passover celebrates the delivery of the Jews from the bondage of slavery in Egypt to the freedom to worship the God of Israel. The Eucharist celebrates delivery by Jesus from the bondage of death to the freedom of the Resurrection.

2) Both Seder and Eucharist are ritual meals with prescribed procedures, blessings and prayers. No one who celebrates Passover as a Jewish person or Eucharist as a Christian forgets the certain prescribed items. And the Christian Eucharist in the Western Church still uses the unleavened bread.

3) Both the Seder and the Eucharist are memorial celebrations. In biblical language and thought, *memorial* (Greek *anamnesis*; Hebrew *zikkaron*) refers to liturgical

celebrations that both celebrate and re-present past mysteries of salvation so that they can be appropriated personally by those living in the present. If you are Jewish, you identify with the first group that was liberated from Egypt about 1250 B.C.E. by celebrating the Passover. You make it actual again by the doing. If you are Christian, how do you identify with Jesus' passion, death and resurrection? You make it actual again, right here, right now by celebrating the Eucharist. What is important to understand is that in the narratives of the institution of this meal, Jesus says, "Do this in memory of me." In other words, Jesus is saying, "Whenever you eat this bread and drink this cup you re-present, reactualize me." This ritual is based entirely on our Jewish roots.

4) Both the Passover Seder and the Christian Eucharist signify hope and the strengthening of the community. What is important to understand is that every Jewish Passover celebrates the hope of ultimate liberation of all humankind from all forms of bondage. Every Christian Eucharist also celebrates that hope. It is an ongoing hope. It is a hope for ultimate liberation from death, hope for union with God.

## Eucharist

*Eucharist* comes from a Greek word that means "thanksgiving." Jesus himself "gave thanks" at the Last Supper (see Luke 22:19; 1 Corinthians 11:24; Mark 14:23; Matthew 26:27). The meal at which Jesus gave thanks was only the last in a long series of daily meals that Jesus shared with his disciples. In the world of Jesus' day, a shared meal was always a sign of hospitality, peace, trust and communality. Jesus proclaimed the Kingdom by sharing meals with outcasts, tax collectors and the like. But this last meal was special. Whether it was a Passover meal or not, it had the same structure. There was a blessing over the bread, its breaking and sharing, and a blessing over the wine and its sharing. But Jesus identified the bread and wine with his own body and blood. Sensing his own impending death, he speaks of himself as a sacrifice. Just as the unleavened bread is broken, so will his body be broken. Just as the wine is poured out, so will his blood be. All four Gospel texts agree that Jesus' death is an atonement and establishes a new covenant. Jews regarded every death of an innocent person as an atoning death, and Jesus saw his own death in this light.

There are clear connections here also with the Hebrew Scriptures. First, there is the idea of the sacrifice of the covenant in Exodus 24:8, 11 and the new covenant in Jeremiah 31:31-34. Second, this is the atoning suffering of the servant of God in Isaiah 53:10-12.

Thus, the Christian Scriptures interpret the death of Jesus as an atoning death that establishes a new covenant in his blood and brings redemption to all. By sharing the bread and wine, his body and blood, Jesus was indicating that his disciples were to share in his sacrifice and in the power of his atoning death. This is familiar in ancient Middle Eastern thought: Eating and drinking express divine gifts.

With the Resurrection, the disciples saw the Last Supper and their own subsequent meals together in a new light. They ate and drank with the assurance that Jesus would make good his promise to be present among those who gather in his name. The new fellowship is now characterized by joy, a fundamental confidence in the coming of the Kingdom. There is an undeniable continuity between what happened at the Last Supper and what the disciples did together at meals after the Resurrection. There is no other explanation for the fact that the disciples repeated this meal and that later communities always referred to the actions of Jesus at the Last Supper to explain and justify what they did at the Eucharistic table. The post-Easter community (Church) convinced itself that it was doing what Jesus intended when he said: "Do this in remembrance of me" (1 Corinthians 11:24-25).

As an act of remembrance (*anamnesis*), the Eucharist not only recalls to mind what Jesus did, but also effectively makes it present again. Thus, Paul affirms the bodily presence of Jesus: "The cup of blessing that we bless, is it not a sharing in the blood of Christ? The bread that we break, is it not a sharing in the body of Christ?" (1 Corinthians 10:16). Those who eat and drink unworthily "will be answerable for the body and blood of the Lord" (11:27). Because we partake of the same bread, "we who are many are one body" (10:17).

The Lord's Supper establishes and celebrates the communion that exists not only between the Church and Christ, but also within the Church—that is, not only "with Christ" but also "in Christ." It is a communion that looks not only to the past, to the Last Supper and to the redemptive events that followed it, but also to the future, "until he comes" (1 Corinthians 11:26). Jesus himself said that he would not drink again of the fruit of the vine until that day when he would drink it new in the Kingdom of God (Mark 14:25; Matthew 26:29; Luke 22:18). Christ's presence in the Eucharist, therefore, is the presence not only of the crucified and risen One, but also the presence of One who is yet to come.

On the other hand, that presence happens not through some magical formula, but through the proclamatory words of faith. The Gospel of John provides a clear warning at the end of Jesus' words about the bread of life: "It is the spirit that gives life; the flesh is useless. The words that I have spoken to you are spirit and life" (John 6:63). The word is ultimately effective, however, only if it creates a sense of community. Where there is no fellowship, where there are divisions, where there is insensitivity to those in need, there is no real community and the Lord's Supper brings judgment, not grace (see 1 Corinthians 11:17-34).

To conclude, we must remember that the historical Jesus and all of the first Christians were Jews who had celebrated the feast of Passover since childhood and for whom it had overwhelming theological significance. If we are to understand what was in the mind of Jesus as he went to his death, and what was in the minds of his first disciples as they reflected on the meaning of his life and death—as they began to celebrate their first Eucharistic meals—we must come to understand the meaning of Passover. In the Seder, Jews of

today still celebrate faithfully and with joy the saving acts of
God throughout history. In the Eucharist, the Christians of
today still celebrate faithfully and with joy the saving acts of
God through Christ Jesus.

## For Discussion

1) *How are meals to be understood, biblically speaking?*

2) *What is the relevance to your own life of what Jesus taught and
   proclaimed at meals?*

3) *Why are the guests more important than the food when you share
   a meal? How do you feel about the concept of nourishment for the
   soul?*

4) *What are the Jewish roots of the Last Supper and the Eucharist?
   Might they have any significance in your life, any influence on
   how you celebrate the Eucharist in the future?*

## For Further Reading

Just, Arthur A. *The Ongoing Feast: The Table Fellowship and
   Eschatology at Emmaus.* Collegeville, Minn.: Pueblo/The
   Liturgical Press, 1993.

Kodell, Jerome. *The Eucharist In the New Testament.*
   Collegeville, Minn.: The Liturgical Press, 1991.

LaVerdiere, Eugene. *Dining in the Kingdom of God.* Chicago:
   Liturgy Training Publications, 1994.

Marshall, I.H. *Last Supper and Lord's Supper.* Grand Rapids,
   Mich.: Eerdmans, 1980.

Neyrey, Jerome H. "Ceremonies in Luke-Acts: The Case of
   Meals and Table Fellowship," *The Social World of Luke-Acts,*
   ed. Jerome H. Neyrey. Peabody, Mass.: Hendrickson
   Publishers, 1991.

Pennington, M. Basil. *Breaking Bread: The Table Talk of Jesus.*
   San Francisco: Harper & Row, 1986.

CHAPTER SEVEN

# The Death of the Anointed One of God

With the possible exception of the story of Jesus' birth, the account of his passion and death is probably the most familiar to Christians. Jesus' suffering and crucifixion have been the topic of many artists and theologians. In Catholic churches, the stations of the cross are a constant reminder of the import of the Passion story. Read each Lent and heard on every Good Friday, these stories are the very fiber of liturgy and personal spirituality.

It is hard for us to imagine the confusion the disciples felt at Jesus' agony in the Garden of Olives, their shock at his arrest and betrayal, their disbelief at his trial, their horror at his scourging and devastation at his crucifixion and death. We know the stories that narrate these feelings and events in the Gospels as the Passion Narratives. All four Gospels include such a narrative. They are dramatizations by the evangelists of the last events of Jesus' life. As tragic four-act dramas, they rivet the attention of the reader on the main character, Jesus.

Act One presents Jesus at prayer (except in John, as we will see) and his arrest in Gethsemane. Act Two narrates Jesus on trial before the Jewish authorities. Act Three portrays Jesus before the Roman governor, Pilate. The concluding act is the way of the cross, Jesus' crucifixion and death on Golgotha.

Because of the dramatic format of the Passion accounts, it is easy for the reader to step into the shoes of the various characters in the story. Often, we feel drawn to participate in the drama and to ask ourselves just how we would have stood in relation to the arrest, trial and crucifixion of Jesus.

103

With which character in the narrative would we most identify? Could we have been among the disciples who fled from danger, abandoning Jesus? Are there not moments in life when we play the role of Peter, denying Jesus, or even of Judas, betraying him? Have we not found ourselves at times like Simon of Cyrene carrying the cross of Jesus or like Pontius Pilate of John's Gospel, trying to avoid making a decision between good and evil or even washing our hands of the whole affair? Or are there times when we are sheepish about our commitment, like Joseph of Arimathea who only claimed he knew Jesus under the cover of night? Could we have stood among the religious leaders who condemned Jesus? While these questions may seem quite shocking, they do help us better to embrace the dramatic character of the Gospel Passion stories.

## Factors Surrounding the Death of Jesus

Unusual circumstances frequently surround the death of a human being. In Jesus' case, the exact involvement of the Jewish authorities is a complicated issue. Early Jewish tradition admits responsibility for "hanging" Jesus on the eve of Passover because "he seduced Israel, leading her astray" (Talmud, Sanhedrin 43a). Yet it would be invalid to blame all Jews of Jesus' day for his death. While some may have participated in accusations against Jesus, in truth it was ultimately Roman governmental authorities who were responsible for his public execution. We must pay attention to this fact, lest the liturgical reading of the Passion Narratives during Holy Week lead to simplistic accusations about the death of Jesus.

What did Jesus' Passion mean to Christians of the first century? The Gospels are our best guide. Unlike subsequent artistic depictions of the crucifixion, the Gospels simply say, "They crucified him," without reference to the manner. The Gospels do detail the dividing of Jesus' clothes and the exact placement of the criminals crucified with him. Why? Such details were important to the early Christians, for they found these details anticipated in the Hebrew Scriptures, especially in the psalms and the prophets.

Theology, not biography, dominated the choice of events to be narrated. By linking what happened to Jesus with various passages from the Hebrew Scriptures, the evangelists tried to explain the rich theological meaning of Jesus' actions. We need to remember that the Hebrew Scripture was the theological sourcebook of the time. Through the Scriptures of Israel, the Gospel writers emphasized what God had taught about the Son. We can see how such an emphasis is an argument against those who rejected the crucified Jesus precisely because they did not think and/or believe that he fulfilled scriptural expectations.

Granting their shared theology, we discern a distinctive insight in each Gospel Passion account.

## The Passion Narrative in the Gospel of Mark

### Act One: Jesus' Prayer and Arrest (Mark 14:26-52)

Mark places the Agony in the Garden at Gethsemane ("olive press"), a secluded grove on the slope of the Mount of Olives. Here we witness the anguished prayer of Jesus before he is handed over, and the repeated failure of his disciples to keep vigil with him.

Jesus takes with him Peter, James and John, his intimate companions. These three were present at the transfiguration (Mark 9:2-13), with which this scene dramatically contrasts. In both scenes, Jesus takes the three disciples aside from the others to reveal the depth of his mission. Just as they witnessed Jesus' glory, they now see him in anguish and weakness as he faces death. To understand Jesus, they (and we) must understand both his suffering and his glory. The true disciple must always embrace suffering.

Jesus' prayer echoes the anguished Psalms of Lament: the desolation of abandonment, the terror of approaching death, the betrayal of friends, yet trust in God's faithfulness. The angst and pathos of Jesus rivet us to the scene in the garden.

Jesus addresses his prayer to his Father. He uses the Aramaic word *Abba*, the affectionate and reverential address to a parent. At his baptism and at his Transfiguration, a voice from heaven proclaimed Jesus as God's beloved Son. Such intimacy is seen here as Jesus prays in the garden.

As the Transfiguration had shown Jesus in his divine glory, the garden scene shows his profound humanity. Overwhelmed by fear and sadness, he prays for the cup to be taken away. The prayer is unabashedly honest!

Still, the bedrock of Jesus' prayer is the Father's will. Dedication to God's will guides Mark's presentation of the life of Jesus. The Son of Man will drink the cup because Jesus understands God's will through his dedicated prayer.

Contrast the ardent threefold prayer of Jesus with the threefold discovery of the disciples asleep. Their continual incomprehension and inability to accept the prediction of Jesus' suffering throughout the Gospel prepare us for their failures during the Passion.

Jesus relates the drowsiness of his three closest disciples to the neglectful tendencies in all his followers. Watchful alertness was to be the posture of discipleship if they were to continue the mission of Jesus in the midst of opposition and persecution.

Each time Jesus prays, the disciples fall asleep instead of keeping watch. Jesus urges them to "watch and pray" that they might not "undergo the test"—the same verb used to describe the testing of Jesus in the desert at the beginning of the Gospel (Mark 1:12-13). That testing, which served as a preface to Jesus' ministry, will continue in the lives of his followers as they struggle with the power of evil in the world. Interestingly, in this scene, Jesus names the polar dimensions in humanity: the spirit and the flesh. The spirit is responsive to God's will, while the flesh is egotistical and opposed to God's will.

After finding them asleep for a third time, Jesus announces that the hour has arrived and he is about to be handed over. Through his prayer, Jesus is now prepared for betrayal and suffering. The disciples, who failed to pray, will flee in fear.

While Jesus is still speaking in the garden, Judas arrives with the arresting party. Judas addresses Jesus as "Rabbi," the honored title by which disciples addressed their master. The kiss further emphasizes that this is a betrayal of friendship. Jesus is the righteous sufferer who is handed over by his trusted companion.

In the midst of much confusion, the crowd comes with swords and clubs to arrest Jesus as if he were a common criminal, though he has taught openly in the temple. A bystander draws his sword and strikes the high priest's servant; Mark's Gospel offers no motive for the action. Jesus does not resist arrest and his final words in this scene set the coming events within the context of God's plan: "But let the scriptures be fulfilled" (Mark 14:49b).

Jesus' prediction that the shepherd would be struck and the sheep scattered is fulfilled (see Mark 14:27). Mark starkly describes Jesus' complete desertion: "All of them deserted him and fled" (Mark 14:50).

Only Mark's Gospel includes the young man who left even his clothing to flee from the scene (see Mark 14:51-52). This anonymous follower stresses Jesus' total desertion and challenges readers to consider their own commitment to remain with Jesus in crisis.

## Act Two: Jesus on Trial Before Jewish Authorities (Mark 14:53—15:1).

The scene now shifts to the court of the high priest for a formal trial before the Sanhedrin, the highest religious court in the land. This council, allowed by the occupying Romans, governed Jews in religious and political affairs. The high priest, unnamed in Mark, presides over the Sanhedrin.

Peter is present outside the trial. Though all the followers of Jesus had fled in Gethsemane, Peter's presence recalls his words at the Last Supper: "Even though all become deserters, I will not" (Mark 14:29). Despite Peter's insistence, Jesus had predicted his denial. We see a hint of Peter's conviction here as he follows Jesus "at a distance."

The witnesses at the trial focus on Jesus' relationship to the

Temple. Jesus has already criticized Temple worship in Mark (11:17) and predicted its destruction (13:2). The discourse of Mark 13 symbolically related the destruction of the Temple and the death of the Messiah. In the trial, the witnesses cast Jesus as the one who will destroy the present physical Temple and build another, not made with hands.

Mark associates each of Jesus' references to the Temple with the plot on Jesus' life (11:18; 12:12; 14:1). If the accusation were Jesus' intention to destroy the Temple, his arrest and trial would be a natural consequence. The witnesses fail to agree, however, and Jesus neither admits nor denies their accusation.

Mark allows the accusation to remain ambiguous. On one level, the statement is clearly a false witness to Jesus' ministry. Jesus is not a militant who intends to destroy the Temple but the Messiah who will himself be destroyed. Yet, on another level, the messianic ministry and death of Jesus destroy the efficacy of the Temple and establish the new spiritual temple: the Christian community.

While high priest and Sanhedrin may interpret destruction of the Temple as a revolutionary claim, the promise to rebuild it is a Messianic declaration. Jewish literature at the time of Jesus held an expectation that the Messiah would establish a new and transformed Temple for authentic worship. We can see how the Gospel of Mark relates the destruction and renewal of the Temple to the death and resurrection of Jesus.

The climax of the trial comes when the high priest asks Jesus: "Are you the Messiah, the son of the Blessed One?" (Mark 14:61b). Jesus immediately gives the response, "I am."

The high priest dramatically tears his garments and labels the prophecy blasphemy. (King Hezekiah tore his garments as a response to blasphemy in 2 Kings 19:1.) The Sanhedrin unanimously and unhesitatingly condemns Jesus as deserving to die. The scene ends as they mock Jesus as a false prophet—even as one of his prophecies finds fulfillment in the courtyard below: Peter denies knowing Jesus.

Mark creates a compelling contrast when he frames the scene of Jesus before the Sanhedrin with Peter in the courtyard. As Jesus boldly confesses his Messiahship, Peter cowardly denies him. The accusations that Peter knew Jesus spread from a private question by the young servant girl to a confrontation with all the bystanders. Peter's denials begin as an evasive misunderstanding but develop into frenzied cursing and sworn rejection of his relationship with Jesus. The second cock crow is the dreadful reminder that causes Peter to weep with remorse. Now Jesus, abandoned by the last disciple, faces his Passion alone.

Mark's Gospel does not try to hide the embarrassing story of Peter. Writing in and to a community that was undergoing persecution, Peter's failure became both a warning against unfaithful discipleship and a message of hope for those who had failed and needed reconciliation.

### Act Three: Jesus Before the Roman Governor (Mark 15:2-20)

Before the Roman governor the trial turns from a religious to a political hearing. Though the Jewish officials hand Jesus over, the Roman authorities will put him to death. Only Rome has the power of capital punishment.

Pilate's role must have been well known to Mark's readers, since Mark mentions him without introduction. He was the Roman procurator of Judea from 26-35 C.E. is questioning of Jesus parallels that of the high priest, except that Pilate stresses the political side of the issues.

He immediately asks Jesus if he is the King of the Jews. This parallels the high priest's religious question: "Are you the Messiah, the son of the Blessed One?" (Mark 14:61). Instead of the affirmative response he gave to the Sanhedrin, Jesus answers ambiguously, "You say so." He does not fully claim the title because of its exalted political connotations, yet neither does he deny it; his kingship is a fundamental truth of his identity.

Jesus gives no further response. Like the righteous suffering servant (Isaiah 53:7), he will remain silent until the final lament at his death. Jesus becomes the model for those who suffer unjustly. He warned his followers at his final discourse that they could be handed over to the courts and arraigned before governors and kings (Mark 13:9). Subsequent disciples of Jesus must be prepared to endure the same for the Gospel.

Pilate is reluctant to condemn Jesus and seems not to believe the charge, but the crowd pressures him. At first he tries to make use of a custom of releasing a prisoner at Passover, a concession to the Jews by the Roman government. He offers the crowd a choice between Barabbas and Jesus. They ask him to release Barabbas, whose name literally means "son of the father," providing an ironic choice between him and the true son of the Father, Jesus.

Pilate is now forced to sentence Jesus to death. Crucifixion is a Roman penalty used against criminals, runaway slaves and political insurgents. In Roman eyes, Jesus is a political insurgent. If the Jews had put Jesus to death it would have been by stoning, since that was the punishment for blasphemy (see Levi 24:16).

Judas had handed Jesus over to the chief priest, the chief priest had handed him over to Pilate and now Pilate hands Jesus over to be crucified. The disciple, the Jewish leaders and the Roman leader all share responsibility for Jesus' death.

Once in the hands of the Roman soldiers, Jesus is mocked (Mark 15:16-20). The mockery continues the fulfillment of Jesus' prediction: "...they will mock him, and spit upon him, and flog him, and kill him..." (Mark 10:34a). The Jewish trial ended with Jesus being mocked as a prophet, the Roman trial with his mocking as a king. Again, Jesus suffers like the innocent servant of Isaiah as he is beaten and spat upon (Isaiah 50:6).

The purple cloak placed on Jesus is the color of royal garments, and the crown of thorns mocks the claim to kingship. The taunts of the soldiers take up the accusation of the trial, "King of the Jews." Irony pervades the scene because what the soldiers say is true, but on a level they cannot comprehend. Jesus is worthy of their homage, but the true nature of his kingship is hidden in lowly suffering.

## Act Four: The Way of the Cross, Crucifixion, Death and Burial (Mark 15:21-47)

Mark's way of the cross is quite dramatic (Mark 15:21-32). At first, the reader encounters Simon of Cyrene, who is conscripted to help Jesus carry the cross. Simon was probably a Diaspora Jew who had come to Jerusalem from Cyrene in northern Africa for Passover. He and his sons, Alexander and Rufus, may later have become Christians, since the Christian community knew their names. "Carry [take up] his cross" are the same words Jesus used when first teaching his disciples about the way of suffering: "If any want to become my followers, let them deny themselves and take up their cross and follow me" (Mark 8:34b). Simon's action is a reminder to Mark's community of the way of discipleship.

Crucifixions took place outside the walls of the city, so the Roman guards would have led Jesus out the city gate. Mark preserves the Aramaic name, Golgotha, for the place of execution, though he translates it for his audience as "Place of the Skull." The name most likely refers to the shape of the hill—it looks like a skull—and to the executions that were a common occurrence there.

Giving wine drugged with myrrh to Jesus was probably an act of mercy; it helped deaden pain. Such an action is described in Proverbs 31:6. Although the mixture was meant to relieve pain, Mark notes that Jesus refused it, emphasizing the full extent of his suffering.

Mark describes the crucifixion of Jesus as a fact, giving no details of the method or the physical agony. He emphasizes the details surrounding the crucifixion: the dividing of Jesus' garments and the mockery.

The Christian community looked to the Hebrew Scriptures as prophecies of Jesus' suffering and as avenues to understanding the meaning of his death. Psalm 22 seems to have been particularly important as a foreshadowing of the events surrounding the crucifixion. Mark quotes several of its verses or alludes to them in this section: the act of crucifixion (22:17), the casting of lots for his garments (22:18) and the mockery of the crowds (22:8-9).

The charge against Jesus and the mockery again recall his true identity and his Messianic mission. The inscription of the charge, "The King of the Jews," meant as a humiliation, ironically states the truth of Jesus' identity.

Those crucified with Jesus are traditionally called thieves. Yet the Greek term also means "revolutionaries" or "bandits," and it is more probable that the Romans crucified them for political insurrection against the Roman occupation. Symbolically, the two, "one on his right and one on his left," become Jesus' royal court. When James and John had asked for the places of honor in the kingdom, "one at your right hand and one at your left," Jesus promised them instead a share in his Passion (see Mark 10:35-40). Here Mark again reminds his readers that the places of honor in the kingdom belong to those who share in the cross.

In Mark, three distinct groups mock Jesus. (1) Those passing by raise the charge of the Sanhedrin trial: that Jesus will destroy the Temple. They challenge him to save himself by coming down from the cross. (2) The religious leaders continue the charge from his trial and mock his pretension to be "the Messiah, the King of Israel." "He saves others; he cannot save himself" is ironically true concerning Jesus' mission: "For those who want to save their life will lose it, and those who lose their life for my sake, and for the sake of the gospel, will save it" (8:35). The mocking challenge to come down from the cross that they might believe encapsulates the temptation of the entire Gospel: Only a Messiah without the cross is believable. (3) Even those crucified with Jesus mock him from the cross. Mark's purpose is to show that all levels of society—ordinary observers, religious leaders, criminals—revile Jesus. He is rejected, abandoned, left totally alone to face his death.

Mark further dramatizes the death of Jesus by having the crucifixion consist of three periods of three hours each. At 9:00 a.m. (the third hour), Jesus is crucified; at noon (the sixth hour), darkness comes over the land; at 3 p.m. (the ninth hour), Jesus dies.

The darkness that comes over the land recalls the

prophesies of Amos 8—9; Joel 2:10; Isaiah 13:10. This association of Jesus' death with the apocalyptic Day of the Lord emphasizes its cosmic consequences. It also reminds us of the darkness present before creation and at the ninth plague of Egypt. As the darkness preceded God's creating and saving acts, so, too, it precedes the saving death of Jesus.

The great cry of Jesus, "My God, my God, why have you forsaken me?" (15:34) expresses his anguish. All his followers have forsaken him and now, in his final hour, he feels the depth of abandonment and even the absence of God. The cry is the opening verse of Psalm 22, which expresses the desolation of the suffering one.

Even the bystanders mock this final prayer of Jesus and misunderstand it as a desperate call to Elijah rather than "My God" (*Eloi* in Aramaic). Elijah, similar in sound to Eloi, was expected to usher in the arrival of the Messiah. The bystanders' confusion is filled with irony, since Elijah had already returned through the ministry of John the Baptizer. His being handed over, his imprisonment and violent death prepared the way for Jesus' Passion. The ridicule continues as a bystander offers Jesus a wine-soaked sponge. The intention was to revive him mockingly to give Elijah time for the rescue.

The death of Jesus is the climax of Mark's Gospel; it brings to a head the theological themes he has been developing. Mark portrays the moment of death with stark brutality. The other Gospel writers describe Jesus' death by emphasizing his control and resignation; not so in Mark.

As Jesus dies, again the scene flashes back to the Temple. The curtain separating the Holy of Holies is torn in two from top to bottom. Entry through the veil into the Holy of Holies was forbidden to all except the high priest, and he could enter only once a year. On the great Day of Atonement (Yom Kippur), a day of sacrifice, penance and fasting, the high priest went behind the veil to offer incense and to sprinkle the blood of a sacrificial bull and goat.

Mark associates the death of Jesus with the destruction of the Temple. The tearing of the veil is a sign of the impending destruction of the Temple that occurred in 70 C.E., about the time of Mark's writing. Through the death of Jesus, the redemptive significance of Temple sacrifice has been nullified. Temple offerings were for atonement—the meaning of Jesus' death. He fulfills the function of the Temple in a new and decisive way. Through his sacrifice, the obstacles are removed on the way to God.

For Mark, the death of Jesus opens the way to God for all humanity, Gentiles and Jews. The Gentile centurion utters the climactic declaration of the Gospel: "Truly this man was God's Son!" (15:39b). This statement summarizes the theology of Mark's Gospel.

The faith of the Gentile centurion and the women who follow Jesus to his death again emphasize the absence of his chosen male disciples. Those who are faithful—the centurion, the women, Joseph of Arimathea—represent what the Christian community will be. Women and men, Gentiles and Jews together form a community (Church) called to share the humble, loving, self-giving life of Jesus.

Mark's drama of the Passion concludes with Jesus' burial. Mark makes the transition by noting the time. It is now Friday, the end of the preparation for the Sabbath. Joseph of Arimathea asks for the body. His fearlessness in asking for the body of Jesus contrasts with the cowardly dispersal of the disciples. Joseph does what the disciples of Jesus should have done: He courageously associates himself with the crucified Jesus and gives him a proper burial. Mark's careful notation of the great stone that sealed the entrance to the tomb, along with the women who watched, prepares for the account of the empty tomb, which we will discuss in the next chapter.

### The Passion Narrative in the Gospel of Matthew

#### Act One: Jesus' Prayer and Arrest in Gethsemane (Matthew 26:36-56)

Matthew 26:36-46 narrates the Agony in the Garden. Matthew's attention in this dramatic scene is less on the disciples' failure than on Jesus' prayer. Mark tells us Jesus returned three times to find the disciples asleep, while Matthew highlights Jesus' three prayers as he faithfully prepares for his arrest. Throughout his Gospel, Matthew offers Jesus' prayer as the model of prayer for the early Christian community.

Jesus prays the traditional Hebrew lament. Matthew says that Jesus felt sorrow and distress. He began to pray in the style of Psalm 42, which expresses a longing for God in the midst of great sorrow and distress. He then fell prostrate, literally "on the face," the reverential gesture of intense supplication in prayer.

Jesus' prayer is more developed in Matthew's scene than in Mark's, and exemplifies the type of prayer Jesus had previously taught his disciples. He had given a model for prayer in the Lord's Prayer (Matthew 6:9-13), and his prayer in Gethsemane echoes many of its elements.

Jesus addresses God as "My Father," the title that continues the Father/Son metaphor used most often in Matthew (see 11:27). He not only prayed to God as Father, but he taught his disciples to understand God with the same intimate relationship (6:9).

As the scene moves on, Jesus gives a realistic explanation of the overwhelming nature of evil and why it is so easy to fall prey to it. "Spirit" and "flesh" are the two struggling tendencies within each human being. God's Spirit fortifies the human spirit so that one can remain faithful in trial. But the "flesh," human frailty and sinfulness, are too weak to be obedient under the test.

Jesus, through the obedience of his Passion, is the exemplary model of faithfulness in prayer for the suffering Christian community. He remains watchful in prayer as the "hour" approaches. Matthew strongly contrasts Jesus' readiness for the trial by his threefold return to find his disciples sleeping. Throughout Matthew's Passion, the contrasting attitudes of watchful obedience and drowsy unpreparedness will be played out. Jesus triumphs in the face of trial; the disciples enter into temptation and flee.

The scene moves on to the betrayal and arrest of Jesus (Matthew 26:47-56). In keeping with his emphasis on the role of Judas, Matthew expands on the exchange between Jesus and his betrayer. Judas addresses him as "Rabbi." In other passages in the Gospel of Matthew, true disciples address Jesus as "Lord." Those who address him as "Rabbi" indicate a faith response to Jesus that is far from complete. It is the same title Judas used for Jesus at the Last Supper: "Surely not I, Rabbi?" (26:25).

Following the kiss of betrayal, Jesus responds to Judas. He addresses him as "friend," a polite but ironic salutation. Jesus' response, "Do what you are here to do" (26:50), shows he is in command of the situation. In effect, he gives permission for the final events to begin.

Mark vaguely refers to a *bystander* who cut off the ear of the high priest's slave—presumably by accident in the crowded mob scene. Matthew recounts the incident quite differently. Here a *follower* of Jesus cuts off the ear in deliberate reaction. Jesus proceeds to give an extended lesson concerning violence, for which he will not stand.

The force of the captors has provoked the violence of the disciple, a retaliatory response Jesus rejects. He orders the disciple to put his sword back in its sheath "for all who take the sword will perish by the sword" (26:52b).

By rejecting violence as self-destructive, Jesus is putting into practice what he taught in the Sermon on the Mount. Jesus also rejects the violent reaction because he does not need defenders. If the Father willed to save Jesus by force, he would send legions of angels to do it. Jesus freely submits himself to the Father's will because, in Matthew's view, the Scriptures must be fulfilled.

Only Matthew includes the detail that Jesus "sat" in the Temple, emphasizing Matthew's portrayal of Jesus as the teacher of his Church. Throughout the Gospel, the sitting position expressed the authority of Jesus' teaching at the beginning of his major discourses (see Matthew 5:1; 13:1; 15:29).

Matthew concludes this section by having Jesus explain

that "all this has taken place, so that the scriptures of the prophets may be fulfilled" (26:56). This designation of the Scriptures is unique to Matthew. All through the Gospel, he has quoted from the prophets to show their fulfillment in the life of Jesus. He refers to the Scriptures as "the prophets and the law" (11:13) and he sees Jesus as the fulfillment of the Hebrew Scriptures' canon. The Gospel of Matthew understands the Passion as the one climactic event that fulfills the prophecy of the Scriptures.

### Act Two: Jesus on Trial Before Jewish Authorities (Matthew 26:57-68)

Matthew takes the Jewish trial from Mark's account; he alone notes that the name of the high priest was Caiaphas. The ruling assembly meets in his home to pass judgment on Jesus. Peter follows the crowd at a distance into the courtyard of Caiaphas. Matthew eliminates the colorful detail Mark gives about Peter warming himself by the fire. Instead, Matthew states Peter's purpose in being there: "to see how this would end" (26:58b). This has several meanings (end, result, goal), and thus the passage has several levels of meaning. Peter came to witness the result of the trial, the end of Jesus' life and the goal toward which it had been wholly directed.

Matthew notes the illegitimacy of the trial and gives a consistently negative portrayal of Jewish leaders. From the beginning, he points out that the Sanhedrin's intention was to obtain false testimony so that Jesus could be put to death.

Mark says that the witnesses were false and did not agree. Matthew implies that the two witnesses are true: They agree on Jesus' words that he would both destroy and rebuild the Temple. Jesus' Messianic power extends to the Temple itself. Jesus had stated his authority earlier in the Gospel: "I tell you, something greater than the temple is here" (12:6). The Temple in Jerusalem had already been destroyed (70 C.E.) at the time Matthew wrote his Gospel. The statement here by the witnesses is not so much about physical destruction, but about Jesus' Messianic identity.

The questions put to Jesus by the high priest concern Jesus' identity as "Christ" and "Son of God." Throughout the Gospel, Matthew has developed these titles to proclaim the true identity of Jesus. With the title "Christ," Matthew has shown Jesus to be Israel's Messiah proclaimed by the prophets. "Son of God" shows Jesus' unique intimacy with God and with his divine authority. Thus, the high priest's question summarizes the major understandings of Jesus developed in Matthew's Gospel.

The high priest asks his question in total disbelief, and Jesus does not answer him directly because of the limited understanding of those titles. Jesus responds in the same way he responded to Judas in 26:25: "You have said so."

Following the high priest's dramatic gesture of tearing his clothes, the Sanhedrin judges that Jesus deserves death. The prophet Jeremiah was also judged worthy of death because he prophesied that the Temple would be destroyed (see Jeremiah 26:8, 11). The Sanhedrin does not formally condemn Jesus during this night session. Matthew makes it clear that it was the Sanhedrin that began to mock Jesus as a false prophet. The mockery focuses on his Messiahship, the central issue at the Jewish trial, while the Roman trial will condemn him for a political crime.

Jesus' trial is followed by Peter's denial (26:69-75). Matthew adds drama to the account as the threefold denial gradually escalates in this scene. First, Peter claims that he does not know what the maid is talking about. Questioned by another young woman, he explicitly denies that he knows Jesus. When the bystanders come over to accuse him, Peter begins to curse and swear as he denies any knowledge of Jesus.

The accusation made against Peter is that he was "with Jesus." It is the bond between Jesus and his disciples, a relationship built up through many experiences, that Peter denies in his moment of weakness.

Matthew alone notes that Peter denies Jesus "in front of everyone." Throughout his Gospel, Matthew stresses the importance of public witness as an essential aspect of discipleship. In speaking of their mission, Jesus said: "Everyone therefore who acknowledges me before others, I also will acknowledge before my Father in heaven; but whoever denies me before others, I also will deny before my Father in heaven" (10:32-33). Jesus' proclamation before the Sanhedrin contrasts strongly to Peter's denial.

The cock crow pierces the scene as it reaches a climax. That haunting signal causes Peter to remember his own vehement statements of loyalty and Jesus' prediction at the Last Supper.

Given Peter's central role as spokesperson for the disciples, and rock of the Church in Matthew's Gospel, this scene takes on intense significance. It is an admonition to all future disciples, especially to leaders of the Church. Yet, in contrast to Judas, Peter's experience offers hope. Peter wept bitterly at his failure and repented, while Judas despaired.

### Act Three: Jesus Before the Roman Governor (Matthew 27:11-31)

After Jesus is led away to Pilate (27:1-2), Matthew narrates the fate of Judas (27:3-10)—the only evangelist to do so. Luke tells of a similar tradition in Acts 1:18-19, though with many differences. In both, there is an explanation of the name "Field of Blood." In Matthew's Gospel, the chief priest buys the field and the "blood" refers to the money used to purchase it. In Luke's version, Judas himself buys the field and spills his own blood upon it in a fatal fall.

Seeing Jesus condemned to death, Judas deeply regrets his betrayal. Recognizing his mistake in betraying innocent blood, he returns the thirty pieces of silver.

In predicting Judas's betrayal at the Last Supper, Jesus had expressed the tragedy of the crime: "...[W]oe to that one by whom the Son of Man is betrayed! It would have been better for that one not to have been born" (26:24). Judas despairs and hangs himself. The deed is reminiscent of Ahithophel, betrayer of King David, who hanged himself after the crime (see 2 Samuel 17:23).

Matthew characteristically alludes to the Hebrew Scriptures to interpret Judas's death and attributes the passage to Jeremiah. Yet it is actually a combination of several texts from Zechariah and Jeremiah. Zechariah 11:13 speaks of the thirty pieces of silver thrown into the Temple treasury. Several texts of Jeremiah speak of a potter's flask in the Valley of Ben-Hinnom, where the people of Jerusalem had worshiped false gods and spilled the blood of the innocent. The place is renamed the Valley of Slaughter and made a burial place. For Matthew, the Field of Blood will be a sign of judgment upon Jerusalem because Judas and the city's religious leaders chose to spill the blood of their innocent Messiah.

The actions of Peter and Judas in Matthew's Passion Narrative set up a strong contrast. Peter "went out and wept bitterly" (26:75b), while Judas "went and hanged himself" (27:5b). The failures of these two prominent disciples and their ultimate fate are both a warning and a message of hope to the future Church.

Now the story returns to the trial before Pilate (Matthew 27:11-14). The governor's opening question to Jesus, "Are you the King of the Jews?" becomes the central question of the trial. Only Gentiles use that title in Matthew. It was the title the Magi used when they were looking for Jesus (2:2). It will be used again when the soldiers mock Jesus (27:29) and in the inscription placed on the cross (27:37). To claim political kingship was treason against the Roman Empire, a crime punishable by death.

Jesus' response to Pilate's question, "You say so," is both an affirmation of its truth and a dissociation from the sense in which it was spoken. Jesus is the king, but not in the political sense Pilate intends. Jesus used this response to those who express the truth, but in a hostile and incomplete way: Judas (26:25) and the high priest (26:64).

Matthew stresses Jesus' silence to all other charges. As he has throughout the Gospel, he associates Jesus with the Suffering Servant of Isaiah 53. The Servant bore his harsh treatment in silence and atoned for the sins of the people. Pilate's great amazement may also be a reference to the same Isaian song.

The trial continues and the custom of releasing a prisoner at the Feast of Passover as a concession to the Jews by the Romans is the next scene. Again, the crowd chooses Barabbas over Jesus.

The choice is dramatized by Matthew's addition to the scene of Pilate's wife. She is ironically portrayed as a Gentile pleading the innocence of the Jewish Messiah. Just as the three Magi recognized Jesus in his infancy (2:2), Matthew continues to show that the Gentiles are more receptive to salvation than are the Jews.

The dream of Pilate's wife also recalls the many dreams in the Infancy Narrative. All of them are divine warnings about the fate of the Messiah. Joseph and the Magi heeded those dreams, and saved the King of the Jews from those who sought to destroy him. This time the opportunity to save Jesus is lost as Pilate refuses to take his wife's dream seriously and succumbs to the demands of the Jews.

Matthew focuses on blaming the Jewish authorities and Pilate's dilemma, noting that Jewish leaders handed Jesus over out of envy. It was the chief priests and elders who persuaded the crowds to choose Barabbas and to ask for Jesus' death. When Pilate asks what Jesus has done, the crowds demand his death more vehemently. Matthew changes the shouts from Mark's "Crucify him!" (see Mark 15:13-14) to the passive "Let him be crucified!" (Matthew 27:22b), emphasizing the crowd's deliberate responsibility for the crucifixion. Pilate gives in to their demands only when he realized he had failed to convince them of Jesus' innocence and that a riot was breaking out.

Matthew's Gospel ties this whole section together with the word *blood*. Judas admits that he has betrayed innocent blood. The chief priests refer to the thirty pieces of silver as the price of blood, and with the silver they purchase a field called the Field of Blood. Pilate declares that he is innocent of Jesus' blood, and the people call down his blood upon themselves and their children. The overall emphasis is the innocence of the person whose blood is shed.

The next scene depicts the mockery of Jesus by the soldiers

(Matthew 27:27-31). After the trial before the Sanhedrin, Jesus was mocked and ridiculed as the Messiah. Now, after the trial before Pilate, Jesus is mocked as the King of the Jews. The derision and torment are a cruel and ironic preparation for the crucifixion.

Matthew heightens the motif of kingship. The scarlet robe replaces Mark's purple cloak, the color worn by the emperor, and is probably more historical, since the outer cloak worn by the ordinary Roman soldier was scarlet. The crown of thorns may resemble a royal diadem. Matthew also adds a reed mockingly to imitate a royal scepter.

The scene gradually builds from derision to abuse and violence. The brutality of the scene is in direct contrast to the nonviolent teachings of Jesus. Jesus taught his followers not to retaliate, and he follows his own teaching as he submits to the violence against him.

The soldiers' mockery of Jesus, like the accusation at his trial, ironically proclaims the truth of who he is. As his tormenters kneel before him and hail him as king, the reader knows that he is a king in a manner totally different from earthly expectations. He is the king who is "humble, and mounted on a donkey" (21:5), the king who "...will sit on the throne of his glory. All the nations will be gathered before him, and he will separate people one from another as a shepherd separates the sheep from the goats..." (25:31-32).

### Act Four: The Way of the Cross, Crucifixion, Death and Burial (Matthew 27:32-66)

Because criminals could not be executed within the walls of the holy city, the Romans took Jesus outside Jerusalem to a small hill called Golgotha. Matthew then delineates the role of Simon of Cyrene helping Jesus with his cross.

Matthew expands the inscription on the cross written above the head of Jesus: "This is Jesus, the King of the Jews." Jesus' name becomes more significant, especially since Matthew had interpreted that name early in his Gospel: "...[Y]ou are to name him Jesus, for he will save his people from their sins" (1:21b). Again "King of the Jews" becomes an ironic proclamation of the truth. The two revolutionaries, one on each side of Jesus, again become his royal court.

The mockery of Jesus on the cross essentially follows the same format as in Mark. Jesus is derided first by a passerby mocking the power Jesus claimed over the Temple. Next, the Jewish leaders ridicule him as King of Israel. Finally, the two crucified on either side of Jesus revile him, but their words are not reported in Matthew.

Matthew adds significantly to this section as he weaves in the title "Son of God." To the first mockery he adds: "If you are the son of God, come down from the cross." This condition echoes the challenge of the demon in the desert (4:3-9). Each of the mocking temptations was designed to turn Jesus from his mission. Now, instead of being asked to turn stones into bread or throw himself down from the Temple or worship Satan, the mockers ask Jesus to "come down from the cross."

The addition of "Son of God" passages fits well into Matthew's plan. Matthew reveals Jesus as the Son of God in his infancy (2:15), at his baptism (3:17) and at his transfiguration (17:5). The disciples proclaimed him Son of God when he walked across the water to their boat (14:33), and Peter professed him as Son of the living God at Caesarea Philippi (16:16). A crucified Son of God is impossible for all to accept, and the taunt of the Jewish leaders was the final test of Jesus' divine Sonship. What seems convincing proof that Jesus is not God's Son becomes, in Matthew, the ultimate proof as Jesus trusts and obeys God until the end.

The story moves to the death of Jesus (Matthew 27:45-56). As in all the Gospel accounts, Matthew recounts the physical aspects of Jesus' suffering and death briefly and factually with little comment. The stress is on the meaning of these events and their correspondence with the Scriptures. Matthew expands upon the events that accompany Jesus' death to focus on the central themes of the Passion account.

The darkness that covered the land is a common prophetic and apocalyptic motif expressing divine judgment on the Day of the Lord (Amos 8:9). Matthew's remark that it covered "all

123

the land" points to its additional allusion to the ninth plague that preceded Israel's deliverance. Jesus' cry from the cross quotes the first words of Psalm 22. But where Mark quotes Jesus' words in Aramaic (*"eloi, eloi"*), Matthew quotes them in Hebrew: *Eli, Eli,* "my God, my God." The change in languages makes clearer the reason for the confusion of the crowds as they think Jesus is calling on Elijah. Since Elijah was believed to come to the help of those in distress, and since his name is derived from the same Hebrew word as Eli, the confusion seems understandable.

Matthew subtly changes Mark's stark description of Jesus' last moment. The verb translated "cried" (27:45, 50) is the same word repeatedly used in Psalm 22 and other laments used to describe a person voicing a desperate prayer. Jesus "breathed his last," emphasizing his control over his destiny and his obedient giving up of his life.

The events following Jesus' death in the Gospel of Matthew help to interpret the meaning of his death. Except for the tearing of the veil to the entrance of the sanctuary, the miraculous signs are Matthew's unique contribution and reflect his interest in the fulfillment of Scripture. The earthquake, the opening of the tombs and the appearance of the saints are all apocalyptic events prophesied for the end of the age.

In the Hebrew Scriptures, the quaking of the earth signals God's presence and power. In his apocalyptic discourse, Jesus speaks of earthquakes as a sign marking "the beginning of the birth pangs" (see 24:7-8). They are a common sign in Jewish literature to show the shaking of the old world and the breaking in of God's Kingdom.

The earthquake leads to the splitting of the rocks and the liberation of the holy ones (the saints) from their rock tombs. The resurrection of the dead marks the beginning of the new age ushered in by the death and resurrection of Jesus. The opening of the graves alludes to the prophecy of Ezekiel: "And you shall know that I am the LORD, when I open your graves, and bring you up from your graves, O my people" (Ezekiel 37:13). The Resurrection marks a beginning and the recognition of God's presence.

The saints who were raised represent the holy ones of the Hebrew Scriptures. Although the death/resurrection of Jesus brings forth a new people, God does not forsake the saints of Israel. Matthew points out that the Resurrection of Jesus precedes the appearance of the saints in Jerusalem.

The climactic confession of Christian faith is made not only by the centurion, as in Mark's account, but also by those keeping watch over Jesus with him. Matthew makes it clear that this is the opening of faith to the Gentiles. Again, Psalm 22 influences the final scene as Matthew shows the scope of the salvation won by Jesus:

> For dominion belongs to the LORD,
>     and he rules over the nations (Psalm 22:28).

Matthew's Passion Narrative ends with the burial of Jesus (Matthew 27:57-61). Matthew abbreviates the account of the burial but gives a few additional details. He does not call Joseph "a distinguished member of the council," probably to disassociate him from the trial of Jesus. Instead, Matthew says that Joseph of Arimathea was a rich man and a disciple of Jesus.

The details added by Matthew show the devotion of Joseph, who remained faithful to Jesus at the end. Only Matthew notes that the shroud was made of clean linen, that the tomb was new and that Joseph owned it. The women, too, remain faithful followers, taking up their silent vigil facing the tomb.

The closing scene, as in Mark's account, prepares for the drama of the Resurrection. Matthew adds that the stone that closed the entrance to the tomb was huge. The fact that the tomb had recently been cut from the rock and was owned by a prominent person distinguishes it from the many other tombs around Jerusalem. The fact that the same two women who will see the empty tomb also saw the precise place where Jesus' body was laid by Joseph is a defense of the reality of the Resurrection, as we will see in the next chapter.

## The Passion Narrative in the Gospel of Luke

### Act One: Jesus' Prayer and Arrest (Luke 22:39-53)

Luke gives the location of where Jesus prays its generic name *Mount of Olives*, rather than the more precise Semitic name *Gethsemane*, which means "olive press." Luke notes that it was Jesus' custom to go there. Luke does not focus on the failure of Peter, James and John to keep watch as the other Gospels do, but on Jesus' withdrawal from all his disciples.

Jesus' exhortation to his disciples, "Pray that you may not come into the time of trial" occurs at both the beginning and the end of the scene, forming a frame for his own prayer. It is the same prayer he taught them in the Our Father: "[D]o not bring us to the time of trial" (11:4b). Jesus' Passion will be the test of their fidelity and perseverance. Again, the disciples are being tempted by the powers of evil, and Jesus urges them to pray so that the trial will not lead them to apostasy.

The central focus of the scene is Jesus' prayer. His prayer is directed to the will of God, and becomes a model for the prayer of his disciples.

The angel is an indication that the Father has heard Jesus' prayer. The angel strengthens him, though the struggle belongs to Jesus himself. The presence of the angel is unique to Luke.

It is impossible to get inside the psychology of Jesus. All we know for sure is that this time of prayer was extraordinarily intense and that Jesus' utter devotion to his Father's will won out over his own resistance to the coming suffering. Luke uses the word *agony* (22:44)—a telling Greek term, *agonia*. It does not mean simply intense pain, but comes from sports or combat and means an extraordinarily difficult but victorious struggle, as Luke's readers would have known. In the *agonia*, then, we see Jesus' struggle for victory over his own desire not to suffer or to die.

At the Mount of Olives, Jesus admits his resistance, but wants the Father's will far more intensely. He does not want his own way unless it is in full accord with what God wants. In this moment, Jesus is fully aware of his freedom to say no to the Passion. He chooses God's will because that is what he wants more than he wants his own safety.

However Jesus' inner mind worked, he has won his own battle before the crowd arrives. The disciples are, if anything, in worse shape by that time because they have been sleeping instead of praying. They simply cannot face what is happening. Either they do not fully believe it or understand it or they deny it in some way. We all use sleep from time to time as a way to avoid coping with the unpleasant or unacceptable.

The scene concludes by contrasting the dispositions of Jesus and the disciples. Jesus "got up from prayer" while the disciples were "sleeping because of grief" (Luke 22:45). Jesus rises because his prayer has made him ready to enter the trial, while the disciples are overcome with fear and distress.

While Jesus is still urging his disciples to pray, the disciple who did not pray, Judas, shows the results of his temptation. Though Luke reveals Judas's intention to kiss Jesus, it does not appear that he does so. Instead, Jesus addresses Judas by name and interprets his motive. The scene shows that Jesus, not the arresting party, is in control.

Notice how Jesus treats Judas: with gentle respect. Jesus does not object to Judas's intention. In Matthew, he calls Judas "friend." In Luke, he lets Judas know that he knows what is happening, but all is done with dignity. Jesus accords to Judas the honorable treatment he offers without prejudice to all people. Luke presents this as a model for all disciples: to treat even betrayers with respect.

Still misunderstanding Jesus' words about how they are to respond to persecution (22:36-38), a disciple cuts off the right ear of the high priest's servant. Jesus shows his compassion even in the moment of betrayal and arrest by ordering them to stop their violence as he heals the wounded servant. Violence is to play no role in the life of a follower of Jesus.

Luke does not mention the flight of the disciples, but places the responsibility for Jesus' arrest on the Jewish religious leaders. In Mark the arresting party consists of *emissaries* of the chief priests, scribes and elders; Luke says that the chief priests, temple guards and elders *themselves* came out against Jesus. The scene ends as Jesus proclaims that it is their hour, the time for the temporary triumph of evil.

### Act Two: Jesus on Trial Before the Jewish Authorities (Luke 22:54-71)

Following his arrest, Luke has Jesus brought to the house of the high priest. Mark and Matthew narrate Jesus' trial at this point, while Luke immediately focuses on Peter's denial and only recounts the trial scene the next morning. This sequence allows Luke to contrast Jesus' reaction to Peter's. Jesus submits to arrest because he has prepared in prayer while Peter fails the temptation because he has not prayed.

Peter's denial takes place in the courtyard. Only in Luke does it occur in Jesus' presence. Though Luke diminishes its intensity, omitting the cursing and swearing, the impact of the denial is just as severe. Immediately afterward, Jesus turns and looks at Peter. This glance starts Peter's remorse. It causes Peter to recall not only Jesus' prediction of his denials, but also his prayer for Peter and the role destined for him (22:32-34).

Peter is easy to identify with: Passionate and generous-hearted, he wants to be good; he wants to be close to Jesus forever. Yet when his test comes, he fails. Peter's failure under pressure reminds us of the ease with which we are knocked off our path to God. Peter is completely unaware that he is "off" until it's all over and the words of his denial hang forever in the air, irretrievable.

Notice Peter's reaction when he realizes what he has done. Sudden tears of intense and honest remorse are among the Lord's great gifts to those who need to know him. When we see exactly how we have violated the goodness or love that we most want, lasting cleansing can occur. Perhaps that is why Jesus let Peter go through the pain.

The mockery of Jesus (22:63-65) is also set in the courtyard before his trial. He is abused as a "prophet," a title Luke has claimed for Jesus throughout the Gospel. As Israel continually rejected and maltreated its prophets (6:23, 11:47; 13:34), now

Jesus will die as a prophet in Jerusalem, just as he predicted (13:33).

The interrogation before the Sanhedrin (22:66-71) does not seem to be a trial in Luke. In contrast to Mark's account, Luke does not mention a night meeting; he says nothing about witnesses; he does not accuse Jesus of seeking to destroy the Temple. There is no formal judgment or condemnation. As in John, Luke describes Jesus' appearance before Pilate as the only trial.

The emphasis in this scene is on Jesus' identity as Messiah, Son of Man and Son of God. When asked if he is the Messiah (Christ), Jesus points to the futility of responding. His response is similar to Jeremiah's words when the prophet was arrested and stood before Israel's rulers (Jeremiah 38:15).

Jesus then utters a prophecy using the title "Son of Man," the one rejected on earth but vindicated in heaven. Luke changes the time reference in this prophecy, radically altering Mark's understanding of Jesus' vindication. Mark speaks of the Son of Man enthroned at God's right hand who will come with the clouds at the parousia (Mark 14:62). By adding "from now on" (22:69), Luke makes it clear that Jesus' enthronement in glory is the result of his Passion and Resurrection.

Jesus is the only witness. In Luke, there is no charge of blasphemy, no guilty verdict, no condemnation to death. But by letting the elders speak with one voice, Luke dramatizes Israel's solemn rejection of Jesus as God's prophet.

Luke's story of Jesus before the Sanhedrin is shorter and not quite so harsh. Jesus is not silent, but neither does he directly answer the question about Messiahship. The Sanhedrin goes directly to the point for which Jesus was finally condemned in all three Synoptics: blasphemy. In Judea, blasphemy was punishable by death—specifically, by stoning. The leaders of the Sanhedrin are not inclined to stone Jesus. Perhaps they assume that if Pilate orders him killed, the people will not blame their leaders.

**Act Three: Jesus Before the Roman Governor and Herod (Luke 23:1-25)**

Luke expands the narrative of the trial by carefully laying out three charges leveled against Jesus: (1) "Misleading our people" is a generic accusation referring to Jesus' teachings. (2) Opposing the payment of taxes to Caesar is clearly false, since Jesus had openly endorsed paying to Caesar what was Caesar's (20:25). (3) The third charge recalls the proclamation of Jesus as king during his triumphal entry into Jerusalem (19:38) on Palm Sunday.

Pilate reduces his personal inquiry to one question: "Are you the king of the Jews?" Jesus gives the same ambiguous response found in all the Gospels. Then Pilate dismisses the charges, finding Jesus "not guilty." This is the first of three declarations of Jesus' innocence by Pilate in Luke.

When the scene shifts from the Sanhedrin to Pilate, we are in another world. In the Sanhedrin, Jesus was among his own people, who shared with him a common religious and cultural tradition. Pilate represented the Romans, who had almost nothing in common with the Jews. The accusations against Jesus at the Sanhedrin were religious; before Pilate, they are intentionally political—Pilate has no interest in religious questions.

In the Synoptics, Jesus says almost nothing before Pilate. He offers only a few affirmative words, then keeps silence for the rest of the scene. Jesus does not answer accusations against him. In Luke, the accent seems to lie on the injustice of the proceedings. Anyone who has read Luke up to this point knows that the charges made in Luke 23:2-5 are simply not true. Jesus did not say that one should not pay taxes; he did not say that he was a political king. Though he surely aroused people, it was for goodness and for love, not for sedition. Though Pilate does not know Jesus' story, he sees that the charges are false.

The questioning by Pilate, in contrast to the appearance before the Sanhedrin, occurs within a crowd of people. We do not know who they are or even exactly where this "trial" took place. Crowds gathered easily in Jerusalem during festival

130

seasons. The importance of the crowd here, however, is that all three Synoptic Gospels affirm that the people of Israel did not understand or accept Jesus.

This view expresses only some of the facts. Actually, all of Jesus' first followers were Jews. Enough Jews followed him to threaten the Jewish leadership. That had to be more than a handful. By the time Luke and Matthew wrote their Gospels, tensions between the young Christian communities and the Jewish faith were high, as were tensions between Jewish Christians and Gentile Christians. Christianity was trying to find its identity in relation to its antecedent religious tradition and current circumstances.

Theologically, the crowd's response recalls the Hebrew Scriptures' pattern of prophet after prophet being rejected or ignored. Now the latest and greatest prophet, Jesus, is also rejected. This rejection is a decisive turning point in the history of the relationship between God and Israel, according to the Gospel writers. With this last rejection on the part of the Jews, according to the Gospel writer, God offers salvation for the first time to the Gentiles, who then become the New Israel.

The mention of Galilee gives Pilate the opportunity to divert the trial to King Herod, Tetrarch of Galilee (23:5-7). Herod has played an important role throughout Luke's Gospel. Jesus was born during the reign of his father, Herod the Great (1:5). The word of God came to John the Baptist while Herod was Tetrarch of Galilee (3:1), and this same Herod threw him into prison (3:19). As noted in the trial scene, the tetrarch had wanted to see Jesus after hearing about his reputation (9:9); some Pharisees later told Jesus that Herod sought to kill him (13:31).

By adding this trial to the Passion account, Luke adds another witness in defense of Jesus: A king and a governor now agree on Jesus' innocence.

The supreme irony of the scene is expressed in the reconciliation of Herod and Pilate, previously enemies. Though these representatives of worldly power humiliated Jesus in his suffering, he joined them together in friendship.

He had told his followers, "you will be brought before kings and governors because of my name" (Luke 21:12b).

Pilate gathers a representative assembly of Israel and summarizes the legal proceedings: the arrest, the accusations, the investigation, Pilate's verdict supported by Herod and the acquittal. Assuring the crowd of the legality of the proceedings, Pilate solemnly declares that Jesus has done nothing to deserve death. He decides to discipline Jesus, Luke's only hint of the brutal scourging, and then release him (Luke 23:13-16).

Pilate's decision to release Jesus turns the crowd into a shouting mob. They call for the release of Barabbas and for the crucifixion of Jesus. Pilate continues to defend Jesus and declares his innocence for the third time. Yet Pilate is not strong enough and the crowd's persistence causes him to yield to their demands.

Luke's account of the Barabbas incident is the shortest in the Gospels. Luke notes twice that Barabbas's crimes were rebellion and murder. The trial of Jesus becomes the trial of Israel as they clearly reject Jesus and choose murderous rebellion. In Luke, Pilate never condemns Jesus to die, but hands him over to the mob "to deal with as they wished."

The people reject Jesus and choose Barabbas to be set free. (Note again the irony of his name. *Barabbas* means "son of Abba," or "son of the father.") Barabbas was a revolutionary, jailed for murder and for insurrection. So the choice was not only a choice between condemned men but between ways of life: to follow Jesus' way of love and inner power, or the way of nationalism, violence and external power symbolized by Barabbas. The crowd's choice was clear. In Barabbas, they may have seen a national hero in chains.

### Act Four: The Way of the Cross, Crucifixion, Death and Burial (Luke 23:26-56)

Luke continues the Passion Narrative with an extended explanation of events on the way to Golgotha. We can presume that Jesus was breaking down under the weight of the cross, so Simon was forced to help him carry it. Luke's literary pen is evident here as he adds, "behind Jesus." Simon, then, becomes an image of discipleship for all of us as he takes up the cross and follows Jesus (see 9:23; 14:27).

The women of Jerusalem console Jesus. In Luke's Gospel, the women represent the people of Jerusalem and become the recipients of Jesus' final prophecy of the city's destruction. Jesus wept over Jerusalem when he first entered it; now, as he finally leaves, he tells the women to weep for the city. Jeremiah had exhorted the women of Jerusalem to such weeping as God threatened judgment on Jerusalem (Jeremiah 9:16-20).

Throughout Luke's Gospel "the coming days" refer to the destruction of Jerusalem. As Jesus entered Jerusalem, he spoke of its coming destruction "because you did not recognize the time of your visitation from God" (19:44b). Jesus spoke of Jerusalem surrounded by armies and trampled underfoot by the Gentiles, "for these are days of vengeance." In his final oracle, Jesus prophesies the fate that awaits the inhabitants of Jerusalem because of their rejection of him (see 21:20-24).

The harsh prophecy echoes the words of Hosea 10:8. In this passage, the people of Samaria ask the mountains and hills to protect them. They seek to hide from God's wrath and escape punishment for their deeds.

By the time Luke wrote the Gospel, the Jewish war of 66 to 70 C.E. was over. The Romans had devastated Jerusalem and the Temple. Luke's community, therefore, would have instantly recognized that Jesus' prediction about Jerusalem was fulfilled. They probably interpreted it as God's judgment on the city that could have glorified the Messiah but rejected him instead.

Finally, Luke notes that two others were led away with Jesus for execution. Luke uses a word that means "criminals," rather than the more specific term "robbers" or "revolutionaries" found in Mark and Matthew. Thus the prophecy recalled in Luke 22:37b is fulfilled, "And he was counted among the lawless" (see Isaiah 53:12).

Jesus' forgiveness of his executioners is totally consistent

133

with Luke's writing. Jesus is portrayed as the great forgiver in this Gospel.

He is ridiculed by three very different strata of society: the rulers, the soldiers and a criminal. The group is inclusive, with both Jewish leaders and Gentile soldiers joining in the mockery. The content of each mockery is the same: Though Jesus claims to be the Messiah, he cannot save himself. They ridicule both his identity and his mission.

The contrast between the criminal on his right and the one on his left is strong and dramatic, representing the conflicting judgments that people will continue to make about Jesus. While pointing again to Jesus' innocence, Luke shows his saving mercy in this climactic scene. Unlike those who taunt Jesus, one criminal recognizes Jesus' kingship and asks for a share in his Kingdom. Jesus promises the man a share in his victory, thus stressing the saving effects of Jesus' death.

The verbal exchange between the two criminals and Jesus is unique to Luke. He tells the story to reveal again that Jesus responds to the honest, repentant person who recognizes his or her wrongs and asks for compassion. Notice that the criminal Jesus forgives will have no chance to "make up" for his wrongs. He is simply compassionate to Jesus and just in his estimate of himself. The criminal commends himself to the mercy of the Lord.

Luke thus affirms that in his very dying, Jesus still offers immediate transformation and salvation to those who long for it. In the midst of mocking rejection and in great pain, Jesus' compassion dominates everything else.

Luke's account of Jesus' death (23:44-49) differs significantly from Mark's. The darkness and the rending of the temple veil (23:44-45) add a cosmic, apocalyptic dimension to Jesus' death. Luke relates this scene to Jesus' premonition concerning evil's "hour" and the "power of darkness" (22:53). Luke explains the darkness by saying that the sun's light failed. The darkness provides an ominous background for Jesus' death. Luke also places the rending of the temple veil before the death of Jesus to join it with the cataclysmic darkness. Luke probably intends the rending to represent the new access to God's presence for all people, Jews and Gentiles alike, because of Jesus' death.

Luke does not record Jesus' cry of abandonment from Psalm 22. His Gentile readers would not have known that the psalm concludes with confident trust in God. Instead, they would have interpreted the words as a cry of despair. Luke proclaims that Jesus dies peacefully, "Into your hand I commit my spirit..." (Psalm 31:5). Jesus addresses these words to his Father, emphasizing his filial relationship to God, so prominent in Luke. Throughout the Gospel, Luke depicts Jesus as handed over into the hands of humans. Now at his death he entrusts himself into the hands of the Father.

The words of the centurion seem much weaker in Luke's account than the confident profession of faith recorded in Mark and Matthew. The Gentile centurion proclaims that Jesus is innocent. Luke, however, probably intends more. The word can also mean "righteous," and Luke will later refer to Jesus by the Messianic title, "Righteous One" (Acts 3:14, 7:52; 22:14).

Luke reformulates the conclusion of the scene to emphasize those who witness these events. The people "contemplated" what had happened and went home beating their breasts, a sign of grief and contrition. Luke shows the salvific quality of Jesus' death: The crowd is moved to repent. He also notes the presence of Jesus' acquaintances "at a distance." Luke portrays the disciples far less harshly than Mark; he does not report their desertion.

The Passion Account ends with Jesus' burial by Joseph, a Jew from Arimathea (23:50-56). Luke makes it clear that, although Joseph was a member of the Sanhedrin, he had not agreed to Jesus' death. Luke shows in Acts that many Jewish leaders are sympathetic to the followers of Jesus and even joined the faith (Acts 5:34-49; 6:7). Luke describes Joseph of Arimathea in the same way as Zechariah, Elizabeth, Simeon and Anna in the Infancy Narratives. He is "righteous" and "waiting expectantly for the kingdom of God" (23:50-51). He is thus placed in that long line of faithful Israelites awaiting God's redemption.

Luke omits many details of the burial scene that Mark's narrative includes, such as Joseph's courage, Pilate's assurance that Jesus had died, the stone rolled across the tomb and the naming of the women. He adds a significant element to Mark's narrative by noting that Joseph laid Jesus in a tomb "where no one had ever been laid" (23:53). Just as Jesus rode into Jerusalem on a colt "that has never been ridden" (19:30), signifying the uniqueness of that event, his burial is also inimitable.

Luke is careful to point out the obedience to the sabbath law. Since it was nearing sundown and the sabbath was about to begin, the women from Galilee took careful note of the tomb and Jesus' burial so they could return after the sabbath to anoint his body according to Jewish custom. When they returned home they prepared the spices and perfumed oil in advance so they could observe the proper sabbath rest.

Both Joseph's burial of Jesus and the women's marking of the tomb establishes that Jesus is dead and has been buried in a unique tomb remembered by them all. Luke's final note concerning the sabbath rest forms a temporal transition leading to the Resurrection.

## The Passion Narrative in the Gospel of John

John is dramatically different in character from the other three Gospels. It grew out of a different community which reflected on the events of Jesus' life in a unique way. Throughout John's Gospel, the incidents received from the tradition are given a fuller meaning; they become symbols that reveal more fully the mystery of Christ and invite the reader to deeper faith. This is true of John's Passion account as well. Our reflection on this account will consider the factors of the Johannine community that influenced it.

### Act One: Jesus' Arrest (John 18:1-11)

John's Passion account begins with the arrest of Jesus in the garden. After the Last Discourse (John 14—17), which has no parallel in the other Gospels, John returns to the narrative of the Passion. He describes the "hour" when Jesus will show his love for his own to the end (13:1). Jesus is totally in control of what is happening as his triumphant Resurrection already penetrates the scenes of the Passion.

Unlike the other evangelists, John does not portray Jesus praying in Gethsemane for deliverance from his impending suffering. Elements of Jesus' prayer in the garden are present elsewhere, however. In John 12:27, Jesus speaks of his troubled spirit; yet with divine resolve, he calls upon the Father to fulfill the process of his glorification. John differs from the other Gospel writers by introducing Roman soldiers into the garden scene. The presence of a Roman cohort and a tribune (18:12) shows Roman collusion in the action against Jesus. It prepares for the dramatic confrontation of Jesus and Pilate, central to John's Passion account, and it reflects the opposition between Rome and Christianity at the time John was written.

When Judas was last presented, he had gone off into the night (13:30). People stumble in the dark because they do not have light (11:10; 12:35). John alone mentions that the arresting party brings lanterns and torches because they did not accept Jesus, who is "the light of the world" (see John 8:12). The ministers of darkness need lamps. The drama of the Passion will be played out in the contrast of light and darkness.

Jesus takes the initiative and dominates the scene. Judas does not give Jesus the fateful kiss, as in the other Gospels. Instead, Jesus goes forth to meet Judas and the arresting party. On one level, Jesus' response, "I am he," serves to identify Jesus, as the kiss of Judas had identified Jesus in the other Gospels. Yet, in John, "I am" also expresses Jesus' divinity (4:26; 6:20; 8:24, 28, 58; 13:19). It is the divine name revealed to Moses in Exodus 3:14. Before the divine presence of Jesus, they all turn away and fall to the ground.

Though all four Gospels describe the violent slashing of the servant's ear, only John identifies those involved by name: Malchus, the high priest's slave, and Peter. Peter, lacking understanding of Jesus' destiny, tries to prevent his arrest through the human power of violence.

**Act Two: Jesus Before the Jewish Authorities (John 18:12-28)**
Interestingly, in the Gospel of John, the arresting party first brings Jesus to Annas, the father-in-law of Caiaphas. The description of the trial is considerably shorter in John. Mark and Matthew speak of a night trial before the high priest and the Sanhedrin, and a morning session before handing Jesus over to Pilate. The only Jewish legal action described by John is the hearing before Annas. This hearing does not seem to be a formal trial, but rather an inquiry or interrogation to see if Jesus admits to anything revolutionary.

At this juncture, John inserts Peter's first denial (18:15-18). John weaves Peter's denial of Jesus together with Jesus' interrogation. When Jesus is questioned, he courageously defends his mission; when Peter is questioned, he cowardly denies his association with Jesus. John shifts from one scene to another as the drama develops.

John is the only Gospel writer to introduce "another disciple" into the account of Peter's denial. This unnamed disciple is referred to several times throughout John's narrative, and is also called "the one whom Jesus loved." This other disciple seems to have been particularly important for the community of John, and is shown as a model disciple in the Gospel. He appears in critical scenes in the Passion and Resurrection accounts: the Last Supper (13:23-26), the denial of Peter, the crucifixion (19:26-27), the empty tomb (20:2-8) and the Resurrection appearances (21:7, 20-23). In each scene, he is shown in contrast to Peter and seems to come off more favorably.

John returns to the interrogation before Annas (see John 18:19-24). John calls Annas "high priest" because former high priests continued to be called by this title. As Annas questions him, Jesus responds with open courage, as he has throughout his public life. He has spoken openly "to the world." Now, his word can be learned from those who heard and followed him. Annas is reduced to silence as Jesus becomes the accuser and Annas the accused.

John minimizes the Jewish mockery reported in the other Gospels. While the Synoptic Gospels contain a scene of mockery showing Jesus as the Suffering Servant, John reports only one slap by a temple guard. John will elaborate the Roman mockery as part of his attempt to expand the Roman complicity in the Passion Narrative.

As Annas sends Jesus to Caiaphas, the scene shifts to Peter's second denial (18:25-27), back to the courtyard where Peter still warms himself at the charcoal fire. The frequent use of the word *disciple* emphasizes that Peter's denial is a failure in his discipleship. The Gospel of John strongly contrasts Peter's courageous enthusiasm at the Last Supper (13:37) with his cowardly denial. While the other Gospels mention Peter's tears of repentance, John will expand his account of Peter's reconciliation after the Resurrection.

## Act Three: Jesus Before the Roman Governor (John 18:28-19:16)

Having reduced the Jewish legal proceedings to a single question asked by Annas, John focuses entirely on the Roman trial. The trial before Pilate is the heart of John's Passion Narrative.

With true genius, John shifts the scene back and forth from outside the praetorium (the official residence of the Roman governor), where the Jews are gathered, to inside, where Jesus is held. Pilate moves from the frenzy of the outside to Jesus' eloquent defense within. This dramatic technique expresses the struggle taking place within Pilate as he weighs his own conviction of Jesus' innocence against the external pressure to condemn him. It also forces the reader to decide personally Jesus' innocence or guilt.

The fourth Gospel fills each scene of the trial with irony. Each scene expresses two levels of meaning, evident to the reader but not to the characters within the scene. The emphasis throughout is on the kingship of Jesus. His condemnation on the pretext that he claimed to be king is the means John uses to reveal the true kingship of Jesus. The true meaning of each scene is often just the reverse of the meaning at first sight.

John 18:28-29 describes the setting and makes careful note of the time. It is the morning of the day before Passover. The Passover meal would be eaten by the Jews that evening. Thus we know John does not present the Last Supper as a Passover meal.

The first scene takes place outside the praetorium. Fear of ritual impurity prevents the Jews from entering the house of a Gentile. They avoid ritual impurity so they can eat the Passover lamb. Yet, according to John, they are putting to death the true Passover lamb, the Lamb of God (1:29), Jesus, who is in the praetorium.

Only John gives the reason for the trial before Pilate: The Romans alone have the right to put anyone to death. Pilate wanted the Jews to judge Jesus by their own laws and deal with him accordingly. Yet the Jews protested because the Sanhedrin did not have the authority to crucify anyone. John sees this as fulfillment of God's plan that Jesus would be "lifted up" on the cross (see 12:32-33).

The scene moves to the inside of the praetorium for the confrontation between Jesus and Pilate. The first question Pilate asks is the same in all the Gospels: "Are you the king of the Jews?" This is a strong indication that the official accusation made against Jesus by the religious authorities was subversion against Rome by claiming to be a king.

In the other Gospels Jesus replies to Pilate's question with the ambiguous, "You have said so." Here Jesus assumes control of the exchange and gives a careful explanation of his kingship. Jesus sees himself as a king, but his kingship is of a different type. His kingdom is not a political reign belonging to this world; it comes from above.

The mission of Jesus is to reveal the truth. The trial is no longer about Jesus' innocence or guilt, but whether Pilate and the reader will respond to the truth. It is now Pilate who is on trial. Jesus is the truth: He is the revelation of God in his person, words and actions. Pilate's question: "What is truth?" shows that he will not recognize the truth in the man before him.

Going outside again to the crowd, Pilate reveals his verdict, "I find no guilt in him." Yet, even though Pilate knows Jesus is innocent, he yields to those who reject Jesus because he has rejected the truth. Hoping that the crowd will relieve him of the decision he is unwilling to make, Pilate presents to them the ironic choice between Jesus, the true king, and Barabbas, a political insurrectionist. By noting that Barabbas was a revolutionary (the Greek word also means "robber"), John recalls the contrast between the Good Shepherd whose sheep hear his voice (18:37) and the robber who enters the sheepfold deceptively (10:1-10). The crowds choose the false leader and reject the true Messiah who embodies all their hopes.

The scene of Jesus' scourging and mockery forms the structural center of the trial before Pilate. It is preceded by three scenes and is followed by three scenes, each alternating from outside to inside.

In Mark and Matthew, the scourging and mocking take place at the end of the trial and are part of Jesus' punishment. In Luke, the mockery is the work of Herod and shows his contempt for Jesus. In John, the scourging and mocking is Pilate's attempt to placate the crowd and prevent Jesus' crucifixion. In the crowd scenes immediately before and after, Pilate proclaims the innocence of Jesus and seeks his release.

Deleting the humiliating brutality recorded by Mark and Matthew, John concentrates on those elements of the mockery that imitate kingship: the crown of thorns, the purple cloak and the acclamation of royalty. The kingship of Jesus is ironically proclaimed as the words of the soldiers foretell the future acclamation of Jesus as king by the Gentiles.

Again, Pilate appeals to the crowd, but this time he has Jesus with him (see 19:4-7). The theme of kingship is continued as Jesus, wearing his crown and royal cloak, is solemnly presented to his people for acclamation. Pilate's proclamation, "Here is the man," is rich with multilayered meaning. Pilate is displaying Jesus as an unfortunate and broken man who should not be taken seriously. Yet we also know that Jesus is the suffering Son of Man on his way to glory (12:23).

The Jews hail their king with the shout, "Crucify him!" "Cried out" recalls that the same crowd had cried out, "Hosanna!...the king of Israel!" just a few days earlier. Pilate has failed in his attempt to placate the crowd. When Pilate hands the responsibility for dealing with Jesus to the Jews, the real reason for their antagonism becomes clear. They accuse Jesus of blasphemy in claiming to be the Son of God; therefore, he ought to die.

Pilate again goes back inside the praetorium and asks Jesus, "Where are you from?" This may have originally been an attempt to rescue Jesus and to lessen Pilate's own responsibility. In Luke, Pilate sent Jesus to Herod after hearing that he was from Galilee. John's Gospel, however, uses this question to refer to Jesus' divine origins. Pilate realizes that he is no longer addressing Jesus on the political level, but is responding to the religious claim that Jesus is God's Son. The heart of this scene is Jesus' statement on power. After Pilate threatens Jesus with his own worldly power, Jesus speaks on another level. Pilate has power over Jesus only because the Father has given it to him so that Jesus may be glorified. No one takes Jesus' life from him, but he lays it down of his own accord.

The Gospel of John shows clearly Pilate's real reason for yielding to the Jewish demands, especially in 19:12-16. The crowds use political blackmail against Pilate by threatening to denounce him to Rome. The text suggests that Pilate bore the honorific title, "Friend of Caesar," bestowed on meritorious officials. If Pilate is accused of benevolence toward a rival of the emperor—in this case, Jesus—he will be harshly punished for disloyalty.

Pilate again brings Jesus out of the praetorium and sits on the judge's bench before the crowd. The gesture captures the irony of the entire trial. Though it seems that Jesus is on trial, the real judge throughout is Jesus himself. His questions have placed Pilate on trial; by condemning Jesus, those who reject Jesus are really judging themselves.

All four Gospels set the day of Jesus' death on a Friday, the day before the sabbath. John differs from the others in stating

this day's relationship to the Passover. The Synoptic Gospels
say that Jesus died on the first day of Passover, while John
says that it was Preparation Day, the day before the feast
began. Though the historical reality is uncertain, each Gospel
associates Jesus' death with aspects of the Passover feast. John
has Jesus crucified at the very hour the ritual slaughter of the
Passover lambs begins in the Temple. The Lamb of God dies
while thousands of lambs are dying in preparation for the
great feast of Jewish liberation.

The final words of the chief priests, "We have no king but
the emperor," proclaim a dreadful judgment upon
themselves. Israel had always claimed God alone as its true
king. This kingship was made visible in the anointed king of
the house of David; the Jews expected that the future Messiah
would come to establish God's reign on earth. Now they
reject their Messianic king and, with dreadful blasphemy, give
their allegiance to Tiberius, the deranged emperor exiled to
Capri.

## Act Four: The Way of the Cross, Crucifixion, Death and Burial (John 19:16-22)

John notes that, as the Romans take Jesus to be crucified,
he alone carries the cross. The Synoptic Gospels make Simon
of Cyrene an image of discipleship as he carries the cross, but
John emphasizes Jesus' control over his own destiny. Here
John continues to show that no one takes Jesus' life from him,
but that he lays it down on his own (10:18). John also wants
to allude to the Hebrew Scripture's figure of Isaac, the
sacrificial victim who carried the wood for the offering of
himself.

The theme of kingship, so central to the trial scenes,
continues in the crucifixion account. As a crucified king, Jesus
is placed in the middle of the two criminals, the position of
honor. The inscription over the cross proclaims Jesus'
kingship in the three languages of the realm: Hebrew, Latin
and Greek. John stresses the universal kingship of Jesus,
proclaimed from the cross to the whole world. Despite the
objections of the chief priests, Pilate insists on letting the

inscription stand as written, a final ironic proclamation from the defiant procurator.

While the other Gospel writers speak of casting lots to divide Jesus' garments, John amplifies the scene with several additions. He distinguishes between the outer garments of Jesus, divided into four shares, and the inner tunic that was not. Though the other evangelists refer to Psalm 22:19, John explicitly cites the verse and shows the two parallel lines referring to different items of apparel. The seamless tunic is clearly the focus of symbolism for John. The high priest's tunic is described similarly in other writings, thus John may be showing that Jesus died not only as a king, but also as a priest.

The undivided garment also symbolizes the unity of Jesus in the Church. While the soldiers divided his other garments into four parts representing the four corners of the earth—the future expanse of the Church—the seamless garment represents the unity of that Church. That unity was the focus of Jesus' final prayer at the Last Supper (see 17:20-23) and is an important theme throughout the Gospel.

The fourth Gospel describes the women at the cross of Jesus differently (John 19:25-27). The other evangelists place the women at a distance looking on. John intensifies the drama by placing them at the foot of the cross and by adding Jesus' mother and the Beloved Disciple. Typical of John's writing, the scene has many levels of meaning. On a purely natural plane, it shows Jesus' care for his mother: He commends her to the charge of his Beloved Disciple before his own death. Yet there are many indications that John has something more profound in mind than simply filial concern and care. Though both figures are clearly important persons, John never gives us their personal names. It seems that their importance for the Gospel lies in their symbolic and spiritual roles.

The wedding at Cana (2:1-12), the only other scene in which John speaks of Jesus' mother, displays several similarities to this one. In both instances, Mary is addressed as "woman," an unusual title when speaking to one's own mother. In both scenes, "the hour" of Jesus becomes central; at Cana his hour had not yet come; here the hour of glorification is upon him. In the context of his approaching death, Jesus spoke about the pain and joy of a woman giving birth (16:21). Mary's maternal role thus belongs not primarily to the physical life of Jesus, but to the "hour" when the Christian community is born.

From the cross, Jesus leaves behind the new community of his disciples. This is consistent with the view of the other Gospels in which Jesus says that his mother and brothers and sisters are his disciples, those who do the will of the Father (Mark 3:31-35, Matthew 12:46-50; Luke 8:19-21). In John, the mother of Jesus becomes the mother of the disciples as the new spiritual family forms from the Spirit Jesus releases at his death.

Many passages in Hebrew Scriptures symbolize Israel as a woman giving birth to a new people (for example, Isaiah 54:1; 66:7-9). The woman in Revelation 12:1-18 similarly gives birth to the Messiah. After her child is "taken to God and to his throne," the woman continues life on earth with "the rest of her children," the Christian disciples, "those who keep the commandments of God and hold the testimony of Jesus." The Beloved Disciple in John's Gospel represents ideal discipleship. The mother of Jesus is an image of the Church, caring for and placed in the care of Jesus' disciples, who become her children and Jesus' brothers and sisters.

John may also be referring to the woman of Genesis 3:15 and the enmity between her offspring and that of the serpent. John's Gospel shows several parallels to the creation accounts: It begins with the same three words that begin the Book of Genesis, "In the beginning...," and notes in 18:1 and 19:41 that the place of Jesus' suffering, death and resurrection was a "garden." Jesus speaks of the offspring of Satan (8:44) and says that his own "hour" is the hour of Satan's fall (12:23, 31). The mother of Jesus, the "woman," is the new Eve whose offspring form the new people of God.

Having symbolized the birth of the Christian community at the foot of the cross, the Gospel of John tells us that Jesus realizes that everything is finished (19:28-30). He can now bring to completion what the Scriptures had foretold about the necessity of a suffering Messiah. His death will fulfill his life's mission, the accomplishment of his Father's will.

"I am thirsty" expresses Jesus' desire to fulfill his Father's will. He is to "drink the cup" which the Father gave him to drink. Jesus' drinking the sour wine (19:29) literally fulfills Psalm 69:21, "For my thirst they gave me vinegar to drink." Only after Jesus drinks the cup of suffering and death can he become the source of living water for all who thirst (7:37-38). Only after Jesus gives the Spirit in his glorification will "rivers of living water" flow within those who believe in him (7:39).

John alone mentions the hyssop plant used to give Jesus the wine. Hyssop was used to sprinkle the saving blood of the Passover lamb in Exodus 12:22. John uses this scriptural symbolism to show that the blood of Jesus establishes a new covenant. Crucified at the time the paschal lambs were being slaughtered in the Temple, the dying Jesus is the "Lamb of God who takes away the sins of the world" (1:29).

Jesus' last words, "It is finished," are very different from his agonized cries in Mark and Matthew. These words symbolize triumphant completion as Jesus accepts his death as fulfillment of the Father's plan. As he dies, Jesus hands over the spirit and begins the new life of the Christian community.

The scene now shifts to the Gospel's attempt to express the meaning of Jesus' death (19:31-37). In each Gospel, miraculous signs following the death of Jesus express its meaning. The Synoptic Gospels surround the scene of the cross with extraordinary incidents such as the tearing of the temple veil, the earthquake, the opening of tombs and the centurion's confession of faith. In John, however, the signs are all localized in the body of Jesus. John carefully notes that the legs of both revolutionaries were broken, while Jesus' legs were not. The legs were broken to hasten their death because the sabbath was drawing near and the bodies were to be taken down from the crosses. Since Jesus was already dead, they did not break his legs. John's interest here is on a deeper level. He refers to the Passover about to begin. The Scripture passages quoted are from Exodus 12:46, which commands that none of the bones of the paschal lamb be broken, and from Psalm 34:20, which assures the same protection from mutilation for the just man. Again, Jesus is shown as the sacrificial lamb who fulfills the ancient Passover and brings to salvation all who follow him.

John alone narrates that a soldier pierces the side of Jesus with a lance, letting blood and water flow out. Many medical theories explain this unusual phenomenon. But John is describing something theological, not medical, hence his appeal to eyewitness testimony. The thrust of the lance shows the witnesses that Jesus is truly dead. And from his death flows new life for all who follow him.

In John 7:38-39, Jesus referred to a scripture passage: "Out of the believer's heart shall flow rivers of living water." John explained that Jesus was referring to the Spirit that believers were to receive when Jesus had been glorified. Thus, the water flowing from within Jesus symbolizes the life-giving Spirit given to the Church through his death and resurrection.

The union of blood with the water becomes clearer in a related passage from the same school of writing, 1 John 5:6-8, which says that Jesus "not with the water only but with water and the blood." It also says, "There are three that testify: the Spirit and the water and the blood." The Spirit could not come until Jesus had departed (John 16:7), until he had shed his blood. Now the life-giving effects of both the water and the blood can touch all who believe.

John's only other reference to the blood of Jesus is in 6:53-56. In speaking about the Eucharist, Jesus says that whoever drinks his blood has eternal life. Blood and water thus symbolize Eucharist and Baptism, the two principal means by which the followers of Jesus share in his life through the Spirit. At the moment of his death, therefore, Jesus forms his Church, delivers forth his Spirit upon it and pours forth the means to share in his eternal life.

The story closes with the burial of Jesus. As in the other

Gospels, Joseph of Arimathea asks Pilate for Jesus' body. Receiving Pilate's permission, Joseph lays the dead Jesus in a tomb because the sabbath is quickly approaching. John, however, adds his own details to this concluding scene of the Passion.

John describes Joseph and Nicodemus as different types of believers. Both were Jews who believed in Jesus but did not yet have the courage to profess their faith openly. Joseph was "a disciple of Jesus, though a secret one because of his fear of the Jews" (19:38). Nicodemus, mentioned only in John's Gospel, secretly approached Jesus at night in 3:1-21. John points to the example of Joseph and Nicodemus to show that once Jesus has been lifted up he will draw everyone to himself (see 12:32).

The other evangelists describe Jesus' burial as a preparation for the Resurrection. They include in their accounts the closing of the tomb with the stone and the women carefully observing its location so they can return to anoint Jesus after the sabbath. John, however, describes the burial scene as the conclusion of the Passion by continuing the theme of Jesus' kingship. As Jesus was hailed as king during his trial and publicly proclaimed king on the cross, so now Joseph gives him a royal burial. The huge amount of myrrh and aloes and the new tomb are elements of a burial befitting a king.

## Conclusion

The death of God's anointed, as narrated in the four Gospels, is not a historical description of what happened but an interpretation of the meaning of Jesus' death. An innocent person, one who has turned his life over to God, embraces as best as can be expected a fate that is the direct result of his prophetic teachings. His followers interpret this acceptance as living out Isaiah's Suffering Servant (see Isaiah 53). They also reinterpret the Messiahship to mean embracing suffering rather than political power. They reverse the image of the cross and interpret it as the throne from which Jesus reigns along with his court, the two criminals on each side.

Scourged, mocked, rejected, derided and abandoned, Jesus embraces death not as a meaningless end but as a means of continuing God's reign in the world. This choice is offered as a model to all of his disciples, who are daily required to take up the cross and follow him. But the story does not end with the meaninglessness of the grave. The joy and wonder of the Resurrection are yet to come.

## For Discussion

1) Why would the Gospel writers present such different accounts of Jesus' death?

2) With which character(s) of the Passion Narrative do you identify yourself? Why?

3) It is your job to ascertain who was responsible for the death of Jesus. Make cases for its being the responsibility of the disciples, the Jews, the Romans, God. Which case do you believe makes the most sense?

4) How does irony play a key role in the Passion stories? Do you see it as a literary device? What difference does it make in how you interpret the Passion stories?

## For Further Reading

Brown, Raymond, E. *A Crucified Christ in Holy Week: Essays on the Four Gospel Passion Narratives*. Collegeville, Minn.: The Liturgical Press, 1986.

_____. *The Death of the Messiah*. New York: Doubleday, 1994.

Matera, Frank J. *Passion Narratives and Gospel Theologies: Interpreting the Synoptics Through Their Passion Stories*. New York: Paulist Press, 1986.

Ruemann, John. *Jesus on Trial*. Philadelphia: Fortress Press, 1974.

Senior, Donald. *The Passion Narrative According to Matthew.* Louvain: Leuven University Press, 1975.

_____. *The Passion of Jesus in the Gospel of John.* Collegeville, Minn.: The Liturgical Press, 1991.

_____. *The Passion of Jesus in the Gospel of Luke.* Wilmington, Del.: Michael Glazier, 1989.

_____. *The Passion of Jesus in the Gospel of Mark.* Wilmington, Del.: Michael Glazier, 1984.

# CHAPTER EIGHT

# He Has Risen as He Said

The Resurrection is the central teaching of Christianity. Paul maintains that "If there is no resurrection of the dead, then Christ has not been raised; and if Christ has not been raised, then our proclamation has been in vain and your faith has been in vain." Paul then goes on to exclaim: "But in fact Christ has been raised from the dead, the first fruits of those who have died" (1 Corinthians 15:12-13, 20a).

No one saw Jesus rising from the dead. Nowhere in the Christian Scriptures is there an effort to describe the Resurrection itself. The Resurrection is felt in its effects, not chronicled in its details. The Gospels describe in two separate traditions the discovery of Jesus' empty tomb and reports (stories) of Jesus' post-Resurrection appearances to various individuals and groups.

The empty tomb tradition appears in Mark 16:1-8 and, with some differences and embellishments, in Matthew 28:1-8, Luke 24:1-12, and John 20:1-10. The reports of post-Resurrection appearances are found in 1 Corinthians 15:5-8; Matthew 28:9-10; 28:16-20; Luke 25:13-53; John 20:11-29; 21:1-23, and Mark 16:9-20, the appendix or longer ending. Apart from these accounts, which are descriptions more of the effects of the Resurrection, multiple passages in the Christian Scriptures simply declare, "God raised Jesus" or "He is risen!" Everywhere in the early Church we find an all-pervasive belief that the crucified Jesus has been raised by God. We will examine these Gospel traditions and their narratives more closely.

In all four Gospels, the empty tomb becomes the important link between the crucifixion and the Resurrection. It serves as the site of the revelation that Jesus has conquered death. The basic story line is that his followers saw his body placed in the tomb before the sabbath began. When the sabbath was over, however, his body was no longer there. What happened?

To answer this question, the Gospel stories appeal to a method used in the Hebrew Scriptures. At many significant moments, God's revelation is conveyed by "an angel of the Lord," a manifestation of God's presence that is a bridge between heaven and earth. Biblically, such angels are seen as knowing God's plan and mediating it to humans.

Accordingly, in all four Gospels, an angel or angels appear at the empty tomb to make its meaning clear. The Gospels' descriptions of the angel(s) vary: whether there are one or two, whether they are outside or inside the tomb, sitting or standing. We can expect these differences in an orally transmitted story. But the angelic message is the same: Jesus' body is no longer in the tomb because he has been raised.

### The Empty Tomb and Resurrection Appearances in Mark

After reading Mark 16:1-8, the first thing we need to do is sort out all the characters in the story: the women, the young man in the tomb and the narrator.

*The women* are the central characters of the whole story, and Mark tells the story entirely from their point of view. They provide a connection not only with Jesus' burial, but also with his entire public life, leading up to his death. These women have followed him, ministered to him, accompanied him from Galilee to Jerusalem and witnessed his last moments (see 15:40-41). Unlike the male disciples who deserted Jesus (see 14:50), the women stayed with him to the end. Their intention to anoint Jesus recalls their previous service toward him and emphasizes their continuing attachment, as opposed to the male disciples' defections. The women's proposal to perform these belated funeral rites also shows their conviction that Jesus is dead. They do not expect or hope for anything extraordinary to happen at their visit. As far as they are concerned, Jesus' story has ended.

Jewish tradition at the time of Jesus was characterized by an extreme patriarchal bias in favor of men. This bias led the Jewish scribes to teach that women were not reliable witnesses and could not testify at a trial. What might be a human standard for the appropriateness of women witnesses is not a divine standard. Now that Jesus has risen, God can choose witnesses to the risen Jesus.

The earliness of the women's visit expresses their keenness to accomplish their service, while "the sun had risen" (16:2) anticipates a possible objection that the women go to the wrong tomb precisely because it is so early. The women can see where they are going. Possibly the allusions to the first day of the week and the sun also have a symbolic value: "The first day of the week" suggests that the women are about to become involved in a new creation and the Resurrection of Jesus dispels the darkness of death.

The women's concern about how to move the large stone from the door of the tomb creates dramatic tension and prepares us for the discovery of the stone's mysterious removal. In reality, these healthy women could probably have rolled the stone away from the door. But the storyteller wants us to know that God is involved here.

When the women enter the tomb, they are astonished by a revelatory encounter with an interpreting young man who announces that the tomb is empty because Jesus has been raised (Mark 16:5-6). At this point, Mark augments the young man's message to the women: "But go, tell his disciples and Peter that he is going ahead of you to Galilee; there you will see him, just as he told you" (16:7). The young man thus commissions the women to share in proclaiming that Jesus is not dead, but alive.

Mark 16:7 explicitly refers to the prediction placed on Jesus' lips in 14:28, "But after I am raised up, I will go before you to Galilee." Mark wished to conclude his Gospel with a declaration previewing the appearances of the risen Jesus to Peter and the other disciples in Galilee.

*The young man* is in the tomb, seated at the right. In the

vocabulary of the Bible, the seat at the right is the place of honor. The Apostle's Creed reaffirms this point when it says that Jesus is seated at the right hand of God—the place of honor.

In the Book of Daniel, apocalyptic or mysteries concerning the end of the world are repeatedly revealed to Daniel through an interpreting angel. When Daniel receives these awe-inspiring revelations, he is consistently overwhelmed with fear and trembling and rendered speechless (Daniel 7:15, 28; 8:17-18, 27; 10:7-11). Mark 16:8 describes the three women as acting in precisely this manner after the interpreting young man reveals the eschatological (endtime) mystery of Jesus' Resurrection. "So they went out and fled from the tomb, for terror and amazement had seized them; and they said nothing to anyone, for they were afraid."

The revelation of the empty tomb's meaning by an interpreting young man—possibly an angel—is an apocalyptic sign that the endtime has arrived and its mysteries are beginning to unfold. The women's terrified response, therefore, is entirely appropriate and expected by the Gospel writer.

At the time of Jesus, most religious Jews in Palestine had embraced some form of the eschatological (endtime) hope introduced by the Book of Daniel. Many believed that when the Messiah came, he would preside over the end of history and usher in the new creation promised by apocalyptic writers. Some Jews also believed that a glorious Messianic Reign on earth would come as a temporal preamble to eternal life and the new creation.

It is understandable, therefore, that some Jews objected that Jesus could not be the promised Messiah because the new creation had not yet arrived. The early Jewish-Christians replied that the new creation had mysteriously begun with the Resurrection. The risen Jesus, they declared, is God's guarantee that everlasting life in the new creation will soon arrive in its eschatological fullness because it has already been inaugurated in Jesus. The Church therefore understands the risen Jesus as the foundation stone of the new creation (see

Romans 9:32-33). The new creation began on Easter Sunday and will be completed when Jesus returns in glory to preside over the conclusion of history.

To validate their conviction that the risen Jesus is the beginning of the new creation, the Jewish-Christians searched the Hebrew Scriptures for proof texts. They assumed that everything God intends to accomplish in history is mysteriously foreshadowed in the Scriptures.

Christian teachers in search of proof texts remembered that in Genesis the old creation was called into being during a period of seven days, beginning with the first day of the week, when God called light out of darkness (see Genesis 1:3-5). They then concluded that God raised Jesus as the light of the world on Easter Sunday, the first day of the week, to signify that the new creation has begun and is hastening toward its completion when the cosmic sabbath begins.

Because of the importance of this theology in the early Church, all four Gospels announce the empty tomb was discovered on the first day of the week at or near sunrise (Mark 16:1; Matthew 28:1; Luke 24:1; John 20:1; 21:4). This announcement is tantamount to proclaiming that the new creation promised in the Book of Daniel has begun with the Resurrection. The early Church includes an allusion to the Genesis first day of creation in the recital of the empty tomb story to remind Christians of the proof text needed to defend their faith in the disputed Messiahship of Jesus.

*The narrator* tells the story to show that death is not the final outcome for Jesus. His primary concern is to convey a new status for Jesus, one that goes beyond death and tomb.

By allowing themselves to be overcome by terror and amazement, the women have failed to obey the order of the young man, "Do not be alarmed" (16:6). This disobedience precedes their noncompliance with the same envoy's command to tell the disciples. Mark states explicitly that the women "said nothing to anyone" (16:8b). The contrast between what the young man commands the women to do and what they actually do could not be more stark.

This fear experienced by the women is the human reaction

to the experience of the divine. The overall impression given by Mark 16:8 is that the women's experience of this young man, his message concerning Jesus' destiny and his commissioning them to relay this message overwhelms and dumbfounds them. Mark uses this strategy so that he can also overwhelm the audience with the Resurrection experience. The Marcan Church is awestruck by the Resurrection. And this is the way the Gospel originally ended.

The original ending concludes abruptly, and the fact that the women leave and do not tell anyone about their experience is perplexing. The women flee from the tomb just as the male disciples and the mysterious young man fled from the arrested Jesus in Gethsemane (Mark 13:50, 51-52). The women's flight emphasizes the ultimate abandonment and loneliness of Jesus in his death. He is deserted not only by his male disciples, but also by the women who remained attached to him beyond his death. Now even these faithful ones leave him. They view the tomb, previously a place of attraction and veneration, as a place of aversion. Ironically, the news of Jesus' triumph over death has achieved what his death itself could not do: the women's separation from their master.

Of course, Mark does not mean that the women were permanently silent and afraid. The added ending (Mark 16:9-20) recognizes that point by showing how an encounter with the risen Jesus inspires faith—not only for the women but also for all followers of Jesus. In each case, that personal encounter accomplishes what a message received from others cannot.

These messages are pertinent to our own lives. No amount of hearing about Jesus ever substitutes for a personal experience of him. Neither then nor now was the task of bringing others to Christ entrusted only to the saintly perfect. Mark's Gospel constantly reminds us that Jesus' first disciples were struggling human beings like ourselves.

## The Longer Ending: Post-Resurrection Appearances in Mark 16:9-20

This section of the Gospel was added later. It begins with Jesus' appearance to Mary Magdalene in Mark 16:9-11. This appearance gives her the courage to do the very thing the young man had previously commanded: She goes to tell those who are mourning and weeping. In describing the reaction of these disciples to Magdalene's message, the author shows that he shares the pessimistic view of Jesus' followers that characterizes Mark. He reports (16:11) that when these disciples heard that Jesus was alive and had been seen by Magdalene, they did not believe.

Disbelief does not defeat the risen Lord, for later he appears, "in another form" to the two of them as they are going into the countryside (see Mark 16:12-13). The reference to "another form" tells us how Christians came to explain why the risen Jesus was not easily recognized. Evidently, however, such a different appearance is enough to overcome previous disbelief, for the two return to the city of Jerusalem to tell the rest of the disciples. Just as they had not believed Magdalene, the others do not believe these two. Thus, the long ending of Mark presents us with a remarkable sequence where ultimately only an encounter with the risen Jesus himself overcomes previous failure to believe.

Mark 16:14-18 offers quite a few uses of the word *believe*. The harshness of Jesus' rebuke to "the rest of the disciples" for their disbelief and hardness of heart is intelligible considering the reason offered: that "they had not believed those who saw him after he had risen." They did not believe the witnesses. The community for whom Mark writes consists of people who have to believe those who saw the risen Jesus, and the longer ending insists that such faith was demanded by Jesus, even of "those whom he also named apostles."

When Jesus makes himself visible to the Eleven, they are "at table"—possibly implying a eucharistic celebration. But the longer ending's account centers on another feature characteristic of the appearance stories: the commissioning of those who now become apostles. In Mark 16:15, it is both startling and encouraging that those who have just been challenged for lack of faith and hardness of heart are now entrusted with preaching the Gospel to the whole world. What better way to show that God's grace, not human merit, is a primary element in the Good News proclaimed by Jesus.

In this text, Jesus makes the promise that "...signs will accompany those who believe...." These signs show the power the risen Jesus gives to those who believe in his name. Yet, since the proclamation of these disciples is "to all creation," the manifestation of that power is wider than during Jesus' earthly ministry.

The longer ending of Mark has developed this third appearance—to the Eleven—at greater length than the first two appearances because the community derives their faith from the proclamation by the disciples to whom Jesus appeared. The commissioning of these disciples is the concluding action of the Lord Jesus on earth; accordingly, in Mark 16:19, he is now taken up to heaven and seated at the right hand of God. Whatever doubts the disciples once had (Mark 16:13-14) are totally overcome, and they obey by going forth and preaching everywhere (Mark 16:20).

## The Empty Tomb and Resurrection Appearances in Matthew

The Gospel of Matthew differs from Mark and Luke in its structure of the Resurrection stories. Matthew frames his story in five episodes: (1) Jesus' burial by Joseph of Arimathea (27:57-61); (2) the placing of guards at the tomb by the chief priests and Pharisees (27:62-66); (3) the women at the tomb, meeting first the angel and then Jesus (Matthew 28:1-10); (4) the bribing of the guards by the chief priests and assembled elders (Matthew 28:11-15); (5) Jesus' appearance to the Eleven and his commissioning them to go to all the nations.

Interestingly, within this structure there are two groups: one favorable to Jesus and another hostile to him. Matthew's unique framing of the Resurrection requires the reader to examine his or her own position in relationship to Jesus.

## Jesus' Burial by Joseph of Arimathea (Matthew 27:57-61)

Jesus' burial by Joseph of Arimathea presents a compassionate action by a previously unknown disciple with the women followers of Jesus sitting in attendance opposite the tomb. This passage serves in Matthew as a transition from the crucifixion and death of Jesus to the Resurrection stories. It sets the stage for what will follow.

## The Guards at the Tomb (Matthew 27:62-66)

Next Matthew turns to the hostility paid to the tomb. While other Gospels end with the hostility toward Jesus expressed in the crucifixion, Matthew carries the theme over to the Resurrection. He uses it to fill the sabbath between Jesus' death and burial and the opening of the tomb. At the end of the Gospel, the chief priests and the Pharisees or elders (27:62; 28:12) work with the secular ruler (Pilate) to prevent the survival of Jesus' ministry. God will frustrate the armed might of these authorities. At the end of the Resurrection story, Jesus emerges triumphant, a lesson of encouragement to Matthew's readers (and also to us).

The posting of a guard, unique to Matthew, ignores certain implausibilities. Three times in Matthew Jesus predicted his suffering, violent death and resurrection on the third day to his disciples (see 16:21; 17:22-23; 20:17-19). The disciples never gave evidence of understanding what he meant.

Here, however, the chief priests know Jesus' prediction, and they understand perfectly what he meant. Consequently, the authorities want the tomb made secure until the third day to frustrate Jesus' prophecy. In the Sanhedrin trial in Matthew, the issues were his ability to destroy the Temple and whether he was the Messiah, the Son of God. Now the interest has shifted to the truthfulness of the Resurrection claim. Jesus' accusers call him "a deceiver" (or impostor), a description that will become common in later Jewish polemic against him.

The skepticism of the authorities and their allegations that his disciples will steal the body (repeated in 28:13) suggests that we may have here an issue that Matthew's Church was facing when the Gospel was written. The Pharisees are noticeably absent during the Passion Narrative in Matthew. They played little direct role in the death of Jesus. They have reappeared here because, in the experience of Matthew's Church, they were the chief opponents to the Jesus movement and undoubtedly were skeptical about the Resurrection.

The message here is the inability of human power to frustrate God's plan. In their attempt to prevent the Resurrection, the chief authorities of the Jews enlist the help of the governing power, addressing their requests to Pilate. Thus, government and religious authorities conspire together against the Resurrection, according to Matthew's interpretation. Despite the use of armed force, neither group of earthly powers proves successful. Sealing the stone and setting the guard will be useless precautions against the power that God is about to release.

**The Women at the Tomb (Matthew 28:1-10)**
In the third episode (28:1-10), when the sabbath is over and the first day of the week is beginning, Mary Magdalene and the other Mary set out to see the tomb. What they see is a stunning series of events narrated by no other gospel. First, there is an earthquake. This is in parallel with what Matthew alone described as Jesus died.

Matthew seeks to convey the wider importance of what God has done for Jesus. When Jesus died with the charge written on the cross over his head, "The King of the Jews," the earth quaked, pouring the dead out of their tombs— something seen by the Gentile centurion and the soldiers with him. Now, to herald Jesus' Resurrection, the earth quakes again. Matthew wishes to signal that Jesus' role from birth through death to the resurrection is of cosmic importance, shaking the foundations of the world and raising even those long dead.

In addition to the earthquake at the tomb, an angel of the Lord descends from heaven and rolls back the stone—again a detail unique to Matthew. The appearance of the angel fits the apocalyptic context: he is "like lightning," just as the great angel who came to reveal to Daniel the last times had "a face like lightning" (Daniel 10:6). His garment is "white as snow," like that of Daniel's Ancient One, who judges the nations (Daniel 7:9). The power of God has intervened definitively at the tomb of Jesus, and before it the human powers who had conspired to frustrate the Resurrection are as nothing. In fear, the guards are shaken even as the earth was, and they become "like dead men" (28:4). This is truly ironic: Jesus lives and those set to prevent that are "as if dead."

The next task of Matthew's "angel of the Lord" is to interpret the emptiness of the tomb. This angel interpreter reminds us that the "angel of the Lord" served as a revealer and interpreter in the Infancy Narrative; so also here the angel of the Lord instructs the women to go quickly and tell the disciples that Jesus has been raised. The male disciples of Jesus forsook him and fled when the authorities arrested him (26:56). Peter, the one exception who hesitantly tried to continue with Jesus by following at a distance (26:58), denied him three times and cursed him (see 26:69-75). Yet these men are still in God's plan and are to receive the revelation about the Resurrection from the women. These women, although present at Golgotha, previously had only a passive role, watching the death of Jesus from afar (27:55) and sitting opposite the tomb when he was buried (27:61). Now the women are rewarded for coming to the tomb by being made the first human proclaimers of the Resurrection and the intermediaries through whom the faith of the male disciples is rekindled. Matthew is surely presenting the women as role models for his Christian readers; they are being invited to go quickly, with reverential fear and great joy to tell others.

In further affirmation of the faithful women, Jesus himself appears to them. Their reaction is interesting. They "come up," awestruck, and worship him. They model how Christians should respect the presence of the risen Lord. Furthermore, the women clutch his feet, a tactile expression that shows human affection for Jesus and proves he is not a ghost.

The storyteller is explaining that a new status will emerge for those who hear and believe in the Resurrection. They will be intimate with the Risen One. They become God's children and thus brothers and sisters of Jesus. Whereas women may not have exercised power before to the Resurrection, the Matthean community (Church) now sees them as fully empowered. Women's empowerment is mind-boggling when one considers the fact that members of the Matthean community are converts from Judaism, where women played no important religious leadership role at all.

## The Bribing of the Guards (Matthew 28:11-15)

In the fourth episode (Matthew 28:11-15), Matthew returns to the story of the guard. Although the chief priests hear all that had taken place and, therefore, how an angel of the Lord descended from heaven and opened the grave, they do not cease their opposition; they do not repent and come to believe. Earlier in the Gospel, the chief priests and the elders gathered and took counsel on how to arrest Jesus secretly and kill him. They paid Judas to hand Jesus over. They also sought false testimony to convict him (26:59). A similar process of paying silver pieces and using falsehood is followed here.

This picture of plotting, bribery, deliberate falsehood and placating the government is surely a reflection of popular prejudice among Matthean Christians. They attribute ill will to those Jews who oppose them. While there may have been ill will in individual instances, Matthew's "the Jews" is a generalization that goes beyond historical accuracy. It reflects wide antagonism and rumors in circulation among ordinary folk—followers of Jesus and Jews—at the time of the Gospel's composition. In the more sensitive interreligious relations of our own times, such a broad portrayal of the Jewish authorities as scheming liars and the generalization of the lie as one circulated among "the Jews" should make Christians uneasy. In other words, this statement is not for all time. Rather, it is historically conditioned by the Matthean community, who experienced hostility from a particular Jewish community at a particular point in history. We cannot use this statement to support anti-Semitism or to accuse the

Jews of deicide.

One aspect of Matthew's story remains an important lesson: He impugns the position that has developed in some Jewish circles against the Resurrection of Jesus. Christians must learn that hostile defensiveness on either side is futile and does little to further the religious cause that one deems right.

**Post-Resurrection Appearances and the Commissioning of the Disciples (Matthew 28:16-20)**

The final scene (28:16-20) shifts from Jerusalem to Galilee. Matthew 4:15 describes the land where Jesus began his ministry and the first call to his disciples as "Galilee of the Gentiles." Jesus proclaimed at the beginning of Matthew's Passion that, although the disciples would be scattered, after he was raised he would go before them to Galilee (26:32). At the tomb both the angel of the Lord and the risen Jesus (28:7-10) reiterate the Galilee directive with the added promise that there the disciples will see him.

On the mountain Jesus fulfills the promise. Matthew does not name a specific mountain, but alludes to the mountain where Jesus sat when he taught the disciples the Sermon on the Mount (5:1) and where he was transfigured before Peter, James and John (17:1). Just as Moses encountered God and received the Law on Mount Sinai, so the disciples saw the glory of God in the transfigured Jesus on a mountain. They come to this mountain again to see the risen Jesus. Despite their dismal history of failure in the Passion the male disciples worship the risen Jesus when they see him (28:17). At the beginning of the Gospel, the Gentile Magi came and worshiped him; at the end, his followers render the same worship.

The motif of doubt recurs in the Resurrection appearances. Some disciples doubt. These members of the Twelve heard Jesus' threefold prediction of the Resurrection during his ministry; they heard his promise to go before them to Galilee and they heard that promise reiterated by the women—yet some doubt. This doubt has a very human dimension, showing that the disciples were not credulous. More important, the doubt reminds readers that even after the Resurrection, faith is not a facile response. It also encourages them, showing that Jesus is not repelled by doubt, for he now comes close to the disciples to speak. Doubting or not, they have worshiped him, and Jesus responds to them.

If appearance stories point back by insisting that the Risen One is truly the Jesus who was crucified and buried, they also point forward to the mission of sharing with others what God has done. These are commissioning experiences. In Matthew, Luke and John, such an appearance makes members of the eleven *apostles*, those sent to proclaim the Resurrection. As Jesus carried on God's work, the apostles carry on Jesus' work. In Matthew 28:18-19, Jesus articulates this relationship: "All authority in heaven and on earth has been given to me. Go therefore and make disciples of all nations...." The wording echoes Daniel 7:14, where authority is given in heaven by the Ancient of Days to a Son of Man "that peoples of all nations and languages / should serve him."

Thus the atmosphere established by the earthquake and the appearance of the angel at the tomb continues on the mountain in Galilee. The authority of the Church is delegated from Jesus, who has been elevated by God and has authority in heaven and on earth. The mission that flows from it will touch all nations. It is entrusted to the Eleven, even though some doubted. We are left to discover whether the word of Jesus solves the doubt, or whether their faith is strengthened by proclaiming to others.

The wording of the mission given to the Eleven is significant: "Go therefore and make disciples of all nations." Jesus already had authority during his public ministry. But when he sent the Twelve out then, he instructed them not to go among the Gentiles or the Samaritans; but go to the lost sheep of the house of Israel (see 10:5-6). Now the risen Jesus, with full eschatological power ("all authority"), sends them out to all the nations (Gentiles). Israel is not excluded (see 23:34), but the progression in these two commands embodies the experience of Matthean community.

Jesus himself spoke only to Jews in Matthew (15:24). At first, so did those who had been with him in the public ministry as they went out after the Resurrection to proclaim the Kingdom. Yet in the first two decades of Church development, they discovered that God's plan was wider. At the beginning of the Gospel, Matthew signaled the extension of God's plan by writing of Gentile Magi who came to Jerusalem—the fulfillment of a scriptural dream (see Isaiah 2:2-4). Now, however, the apostles clearly cannot simply wait for the Gentiles to come; they must go out to them.

Jesus' solemn last words, "...I am with you always, to the end of the age" (Matthew 28:20), echo the words spoken about him in the beginning of the Gospel (1:23):

> Look, the virgin shall conceive and bear a son,
>     and they shall name him Emmanuel,
> which means, "God is with us."

The Resurrection is, for Matthew, not only evidence that God was with Jesus, who conquered death. It also shows that, in Jesus, God's abiding presence is with all those who are baptized and who observe all that Jesus has commanded, as taught by the disciples. In Isaiah 41:10, God promised Israel: "[D]o not fear, for I am with you." Here Matthew conveys the promise to an enlarged people, including Gentiles who have come to know God in Jesus Christ. Earthly powers, represented by the secular ruler, the chief priests and the scribes/elders tried to prevent the plan of God, both at the conception/birth of Jesus, and at his crucifixion/resurrection. They were unsuccessful then, and they will be equally unsuccessful in preventing it till the end of time.

### The Empty Tomb and Resurrection Appearances in Luke

Like Matthew, Luke follows Mark in the basic story of the empty tomb. Luke's account, however, has its own distinctive characteristics. Luke's story of the discovery of the empty tomb in 24:1-12 recounts all the events as happening on the same day—the first day of the week. This is the day that

Christians gathered for the breaking of bread, the first day of the new age, the day they will set apart each week as the day of Resurrection.

Luke notes that the two men who announced the Resurrection wore dazzling garments, suggesting their otherworldly nature. Throughout the Gospel of Luke, those who proclaim the message of Jesus or perform some divinely appointed task are presented in pairs. Pairing is a Lucan literary device. Men and women are paired: Elizabeth and Zechariah, Mary and Joseph, Simeon and Anna, to mention but a few. The 72 disciples are set out in pairs. Similarly, two men prepared for Jesus' entry into Jerusalem and for the Passover meal. Two men appeared with Jesus in the Transfiguration (Moses and Elijah), two will encounter him on the road to Emmaus, and two will also interpret his Ascension (see Acts 1:10).

Luke's pairing of the two men in this empty tomb story with the women, is a sign of Luke's inclusivity. The men begin by challenging the women's focus on the tomb, "Why do you look for the living among the dead?" (24:5b). This challenge is quite similar to the one given at the Ascension: "...[W]hy do you stand looking up toward heaven?" (Acts 1:11). After each challenging question the commission given by Luke sets the hearers off on their mission.

Unlike Mark and Matthew, Luke says nothing of Resurrection appearances in Galilee. Instead, Jerusalem remains the focal point in Luke's writing. Jerusalem is the place toward which the Gospel proceeds, the city of Jesus' destiny and the place from which the ministry of the early Church disseminates. Jerusalem is a fitting selection from the tradition for Luke's purpose. For him, the Gospel began with the appearance of Gabriel to Zechariah in the Jerusalem Temple. Now it ends with Jesus' disciples in the Temple blessing God.

The names of the women at the tomb vary slightly from the other Gospels. Joanna is found only in Luke, who describes her as the wife of Herod's steward (8:3). Though the women proclaimed the message to the eleven men, Luke makes it clear that the male apostles did not accept the women's report since it seemed like nonsense. Only actual experience of the risen Lord will bring the males to faith. Luke underscores this when Peter visits the empty tomb (Luke 24:12). Peter's experience leads to amazement, not to belief, for he has not yet experienced the risen Christ.

There are three post-Resurrection appearance stories in the Gospel of Luke: the two disciples on the road to Emmaus (Luke 24:13-35), the disciples in Jerusalem (Luke 24:36-49) and the Ascension (Luke 24:50-53).

**The Disciples on the Road to Emmaus (Luke 24:50-53)**

The story of the two disciples on the road to Emmaus is the most detailed and elaborate of the appearance stories. It is an invitation to faith. The principal psychological steps in the genesis of faith can be traced in the two disciples' reaction to the risen Jesus. They are disturbed, upset and unsatisfied with the actual situation in which they find themselves. This is the first step in the development of faith.

The second step is a shock that changes one's standard of judgment. This happens here in the exposition of the Scriptures by the risen Jesus. The disciples have, presumably, read and pondered the Scriptures. But never before had they perceived a thread running through the passages that Christ highlights for them: namely, that the Messiah would enter his glory through suffering. This was a new insight that changed the disciples' preconceived ideas. The disciples become more receptive to a new future. What that is they are not clear on, so they ask Jesus to remain with them, to guide them.

Faith is essentially holding in a single mental glance the usual and the unusual; the normal and the abnormal. The catalyst here is the meal, because it provides the context in which the two elements of faith are brought together. It includes the normal: ordinary life, food, words of blessing. Also present is the other plane, which goes beyond normal life, but is also explained as real: the presence of Jesus, who has risen. At the meal, the disciples recognize Jesus—a new act of faith. Faith is not mentioned explicitly in the text by

Luke but it is clearly implied in the disciples' return to Jerusalem and their proclamation to the Eleven.

The disciples felt as if they should have known Jesus at once—again a common experience. At certain points in our lives we look back and see the path along which we have travelled. The way seemed obscure, at the time, with many possible turns. But looking back, the road seems perfectly clear. This was the disciples' attitude.

This is one of the reasons why the story is such a tremendous favorite; it is psychologically true. It articulates the common experience of anyone who has come to faith. It raises certain questions: What passages was Jesus talking about? What was the difference between this meal and others? This text, as it stands, is a clever pedagogic text. It's good teaching. Notice how easily it lends itself to an exposition of the Scriptures regarding the nature of him who was to come and to an exposition of the Eucharist.

The following diagram of the structure of the text helps show what it teaches.

# Structure of Luke 24:13-33

**A.** Two disciples leave Jerusalem (24:13).

  **B.** They converse (24:14).

   **C.** Jesus joins them (24:15).

    **D** "[B]ut their eyes were kept from recognizing him" (24:16).

     **E.** Jesus' initiative (24:17).

      **F.** The disciples explain how the chief priests and leaders handed over Jesus, a prophet whom many hoped was the Messiah, to be condemned to death and crucified (24:19-20).

       **G.** They tell how the women found the tomb empty and saw "a vision of angels" (24:22-23).

        **H.** The angels said Jesus was alive (24:23c).

       **G'** Other disciples went to the tomb and found it empty as the women had said, but did not see him (24:24).

      **F'** Jesus explains Scripture's prophecies. "Was it not necessary that the Messiah should suffer these things and then enter into his glory?" (24:25-27).

     **E'** The disciples' initiative (24:29): "Stay with us."

    **D'** The disciples recognize Jesus (24:31a) in the breaking of the bread (24:31a).

   **C'** Jesus leaves them (24:31b).

  **B'** They converse (24:32).

**A'** The two disciples return to Jerusalem (24:33).

169

This chart shows Luke's carefully calculated literary form. The story is a product of great literary skill directed toward a catechetical (religious education) purpose. The text forces people to ask questions about the Hebrew Scriptures, about Jesus, about the Resurrection and about Eucharist.

To answer these questions, it is important to look at some key terms used in the story. One is the term *prophet* (24:19). Throughout this gospel, Luke has acclaimed Jesus as a prophet. Like Elisha and Elijah, the scope of his prophetic mission includes non-Jews and God's covenant people. Like the prophets of old, Jesus performs many miracles, such as the cleansing of a leper or the raising of a dead son (7:16; 17:11-19); as a prophet, Jesus proclaims God's law and calls down woe on sinners (10:13-14; 19:41-44). In line with the prophets of old, Jesus is a rejected prophet who suffers innocently at the hands of sinful Jerusalem (13:33-35). Finally, when Jesus' disciples acclaim him as "a prophet, mighty in word and deed," the reader of Luke's Gospel realizes how appropriate such a title truly is for Jesus.

At the very beginning of his career in Luke's Gospel, Jesus proclaimed in the synagogue a text of Isaiah that pragmatically described his future mission (4:18-19). According to the prophecy, Jesus was commissioned to be *mighty in word and deed*— "to bring the good news to the poor...to proclaim the year of the Lord's favor" (word) and to bring " recovery of sight to the blind,...to let the oppressed go free" (deed).

The disciples had hoped that Jesus was *the one to redeem Israel* (24:21). At the beginning of the Gospel, God's angels acclaimed Jesus as "a savior, who is the Messiah, the Lord" (2:11). Jesus, indeed, acts as savior in his ministry of healing and forgiving and especially on the cross, when he promises the thief that he will be with Jesus in paradise today (23:43). Luke proclaims Jesus as the unique and necessary savior of all. He truly does "set Israel free," perhaps not from the occupying army of the Romans, but free from sin, disease and death.

It was necessary for the Messiah to *suffer* (24:26). This

revelation is new to the disciples on the road, for they may have expected a military or political Messiah, not a suffering one. In God's plan, biblically speaking, suffering has always been the forte of God's messengers and saints.

By referring to *Moses and the prophets* (24:27), Luke is proclaiming that Jesus' life is a fulfillment of the Scriptures. He shows that the sufferings of God's Messiah are not an argument against his legitimacy. Instead, they are his confirmation as the Christ, for the essence of the Scriptures shows that the Christ must suffer to enter his glory.

### The Appearance to the Disciples in Jerusalem (Luke 24:36-49)

This Resurrection appearance is experienced by the Eleven and those gathered with them in Jerusalem immediately after the two disciples return from Emmaus with their report. It parallels the Emmaus account in several ways. In both scenes, Jesus' presence is misunderstood. An instruction from the Scriptures leads to understanding. A meal is shared and Jesus departs. In this text, Jesus' bodily presence and the disciples' mission is central.

Similarities in Luke and John suggest a tradition used by both. In John, as in Luke, Jesus stands in the midst of his disciples and says, "Peace be with you." He shows them the wounds of his crucifixion and the disciples respond with joy. Jesus commissions his disciples and assures them of the presence of his Spirit (John 20:19-22).

The appearance of the risen Jesus provokes a variety of reactions in his disciples: They are startled, terrified, troubled, incredulous, joyful and amazed. Jesus stands among them with his message of "peace" (*shalom*). This greeting wishes the receiver a completeness or fulfillment that cannot be had from the world but is brought by Christ's victory.

The passage maintains that the risen presence of Jesus is physical. The disciples touch him. He shows them his hands and his feet. He eats with them. Jesus points out that a ghost does not have flesh and bones as he has. He establishes his identity and convinces them that he is the same person who lived among them before his death.

The disciples listen intently as Jesus explains what pertains to him from the Scriptures. The law, the prophets and the psalms are traditionally the entire Hebrew Scriptures. Only through the Resurrection can the disciples see how Jesus fulfills God's salvific plan.

Here, as in the finale of Matthew's Gospel, Jesus commissions his followers to carry out a future mission in his name. The disciples are to be witnesses, beginning in Jerusalem and extending to all the nations. The goal of Jesus' journey, Jerusalem, now becomes the starting point from which the message of salvation will extend to the ends of the earth. For Luke, Jerusalem is not only the Holy City where Jesus' earthly life culminates, it is the place from which the Church moves into the world.

### The Ascension (Luke 24:50-53)

Luke is unique in speaking of Jesus' ascension at the end of his appearances. It brings to a close his account of Jesus' life. The Ascension will also begin Luke's account of the early Church in Acts of the Apostles. Here it occurs on the same day as the Resurrection, whereas in Acts 1:9-11 it takes place forty days later. The essential affirmation of both accounts is that Jesus is with the Father in glory.

Jesus' final action is to raise his hands and bless them. This action is imitative of the priestly blessing over the people given by Aaron and by the priests of Israel after him. As Jesus blesses his disciples, he departs.

The Gospel ends where it began, in the Jerusalem Temple. The followers of Jesus joyfully and continually praised God in the Temple. In this way, Luke begins his description of the community life of the Church and prepares for the Acts of the Apostles.

### The Empty Tomb and Resurrection Appearances in John

To begin to understand the Resurrection stories in the Gospel of John, we must begin by looking at their structure. The stories are narrated in John 20—21. John 20 consists of a series of diverse reactions to the Resurrection: those of Simon Peter and the Beloved Disciple (20:1-20), of Mary Magdalene (20:11-18), of the disciples (20:19-23) and of Thomas (20:24-29). John 21 presents a variety of appearances by the risen Jesus: to the disciples at the Sea of Tiberias (21:1-8), on the shore of the sea with a meal of bread and fish (21:9-14), to Simon Peter (21:15-19) and to the Beloved Disciple (21:20-24).

## The Reactions of Simon Peter and the Beloved Disciple (John 20:1-10)

In all four Gospels, women come to the empty tomb on the first day of the week, but only in John does Mary Magdalene visit the tomb twice. The second visit (John 20:11-17) has major parallels to the other Gospel accounts; the first visit functions mostly to set the stage of the story of Simon Peter and the Beloved Disciple. Even in such a setting, however, there are uniquely Johannine touches. As in Mark and Luke, Mary Magdalene comes "early"; only John adds that "it was still dark." In this Gospel where light and darkness play such an important role, darkness lasts until someone believes in the risen Jesus.

John does not tell us why Mary Magdalene comes to the tomb; but her alarmed racing off to tell the two disciples, "They have taken the Lord out of the tomb, and we do not know where they have laid him," suggests a close personal attachment to Jesus. Her immediate conclusion that Jesus' body has been stolen is unique to John. Mary Magdalene jumps to the conclusion that Jesus' "enemies" have done the stealing, for she reports to the disciples that others have stolen the body.

The two disciples who respond to Magdalene's report about the tomb are Simon Peter and the Beloved Disciple. The "Beloved Disciple" or "the disciple whom Jesus loved" is never mentioned as such during the first part of the Gospel of John, which describes Jesus' public ministry. But the Beloved Disciple appears with startling frequency in the second part of the Gospel: at the Last Supper next to Jesus, in the high priest's courtyard next to Simon Peter and near the cross of

Jesus, next to Jesus' mother.

The Beloved Disciple does not appear in the Synoptic Gospels. In John he has the highest rank because Jesus loves him. John 20:2 uses two titles: "the other disciple" and "the one whom Jesus loved." The first title may have been the way he was evaluated by other Christians; the second title was the way he was known to those who preserved his memory in the Gospel of John.

The Fourth Gospel sensitively paints the delicate relationship between the Beloved Disciple and the famous Peter. The Beloved Disciple reaches the tomb first but does not enter, allowing Peter to catch up and enter first. Neither the arrival nor the entry is the feature of John's contrast between the two figures. The point is that they respond differently to what they see in the tomb. The Beloved Disciple believed, and nothing in the text shows that Peter believed.

John 20:8 relates this belief to what the disciples saw: the burial garments in an otherwise empty tomb. Lazarus came forth from the tomb, "his hands and feet bound with strips of cloth, and his face wrapped in a cloth" (John 11:44). Jesus has left the same twofold set of wrappings *in* the tomb. Jesus resuscitated Lazarus to natural life, but he would die and need his burial garments again. By contrast, the garments left in Jesus' tomb reveal to the disciple that Jesus has been raised to eternal life. The added Johannine comment that "...as yet they did not understand the scripture, that he must rise from the dead" (20:9) explains Simon Peter's failure to understand.

As Luke 24:25-27, 32 shows, explanation of the Scriptures helped Jesus' disciples to accept the Resurrection. Again, by contrast, the extraordinary sensitivity of the Beloved Disciple is highlighted, since this disciple needed no such help.

### Mary Magdalene's Reaction to the Empty Tomb (John 20:11-18)

John 20:10 assures us that "the disciples returned to their homes." The evangelist's dramatic preference for an individual encounter with Jesus has led him to remove Simon Peter and the Beloved Disciple from the tomb before the episode in which Mary Magdalene comes to faith. Neither the Beloved Disciple's faith perception nor Simon Peter's lack of it influence Mary Magdalene, whose reaction the fourth Gospel evaluates on its own.

In describing Mary's second visit to the tomb, John rejoins the common Christian tradition that she encountered an angelic presence there. Unique to John is that he carefully positions one angel at the head and the other at the foot of the place where Jesus had lain—comparable to the careful description in 20:6-7 that positioned the burial wrappings and the cloth that had covered Jesus' head separately.

Readers of John's Gospel are not meant to ask why these angels were not there when Simon Peter and the Beloved Disciple entered the tomb. The Gospel of John is illustrating different reactions. In the previous episode (20:1-2), Mary Magdalene's first impression at the tomb was negative. It served, however, as a transition to the positive main story of how the Beloved Disciple came to faith. Similarly, despite the presence of the angels, Mary Magdalene's second impression of the tomb (20:11-13) is negative ("They have taken away my Lord, and I do not know where they have laid him"), but it serves as a transition to the positive main story where she will come to faith (20:14-18). That development is made possible not by angels but by Jesus himself.

The appearance of the risen Jesus to Mary Magdalene is a dramatic encounter. Although Jesus stands plainly in sight and speaks to her, she does not recognize him. Jesus' question, "Whom are you looking for?" echoes the first words he spoke in the Gospel (1:35-38) when Jesus turned around and found the two disciples of John the Baptist following him: "What are you looking for?" It is a question that probes discipleship. The disciples of John the Baptist stayed with Jesus and found the Messiah (1:41). The hostile arresting party was looking for Jesus the Nazarene. They found him but were struck down in judgment (18:6). Mary Magdalene is looking for the dead Jesus; she will find the living Lord.

Although the failure to recognize Jesus is a common feature in Gospel post-Resurrection appearances, the way

John dramatizes Mary Magdalene's lack of recognition is unique. Her reiterated supposition that people have carried Jesus off and her consuming concern to know where they have put him focuses on the one whom she supposes to be the tender of the garden in which John 19:41 (alone) has told us Jesus was buried. The depth of Mary Magdalene's concern comes in the question posed to her by both the angels and the unrecognized risen Jesus: "Why are you weeping?" This query gives the impression that tears have blurred her vision. The failure to see Jesus is overcome when he calls her by name. Mary Magdalene's spontaneous reaction to being called by name, "Rabbouni!" (an endearing term for the teacher, or better, "my teacher"), verifies her closeness to Jesus.

Mixed into Mary Magdalene's recognition and love is an all too human element. She wants to hold on to Jesus and not let him go. She would hold on to his presence, keeping him here below. When Jesus says to her, "I am ascending to my Father" (20:17c), he is reiterating where his home is: the world above, to which he belongs. When he adds, "and your Father," he is revealing to her that, because of her post-Resurrection faith, the world to which she now belongs is also above, the many mansions of Jesus' heavenly Father's house.

By saying that his Father is "your Father," Jesus is vocalizing in his own words the promise of the Gospel Prologue, "But to all who received him,...he gave power to become children of God" (1:12). That same new status Jesus applies to the disciples, calling them "my brothers" in 20:17 as he sends Mary out to them. If, at the beginning of the tomb story, Mary Magdalene went to tell the disciples that "they took the Lord from the tomb," at the end of the tomb story she goes to tell them, "I have seen the Lord."

The Beloved Disciple was the first to believe. Mary Magdalene is the first to proclaim the risen Lord. In later tradition, she will be called the apostle ("the one sent") to the apostles.

**Reaction of the Disciples (John 20:19-23)**

In narrating Jesus' appearance to the group of disciples, the Gospel of John is close to a common tradition, for several Gospels describe a commissioning appearance. Again, John has his own way of arranging the reactions. Mary Magdalene went to the tomb "Early on the first day of the week, while it was still dark" (20:1). In 20:19, he gives this setting: "When it was evening on that day, the first day of the week, and the doors of the house where the disciples had met were locked for fear of the Jews...."

The darkness has been dispelled because the Beloved Disciple and Mary Magdalene know that the Lord has risen, but fear and hiding still mark the lives of the disciples. The disciples know Mary Magdalene has already seen the Lord; this explains their lack of doubt when he appears. Jesus' "Peace be with you" (20:19) goes beyond a greeting because of what Jesus promised at the Last Supper, "Peace I leave with you; my peace I give to you. I do not give to you as the world gives" (14:27).

In John 20:20, the risen Jesus shows his disciples his hands and side, the wounds inflicted during the crucifixion. He thus removes all question of his identity and fulfills the Last Supper promise, "So you have pain now; but I will see you again, and your hearts will rejoice, and no one will take your joy from you" (16:22). In reporting the reactions of the disciples, the Gospel of John says that they saw that it was "the Lord." This standard post-Resurrection title tells us that they believed.

Jesus repeats, "Peace be with you" (20:21b). This emphasizes that we have here no simple greeting, but also suggests that peace is to accompany the disciples in their forthcoming assignments. The first of these Jesus conveys through the commissioning, "As the Father has sent me, so I send you" (20:21c). This commissioning is comparable to the apostolic commissioning of the Eleven in the Synoptics. The origin of the commissioning is the Father's sending of Jesus with all the purpose that implies: to bring life, light, truth. Just as the Father was present in the Son during the Son's mission, so now the disciples in their mission must manifest Jesus' presence to the point that whoever sees the disciples sees Jesus and the Father.

The disciples' representing Jesus becomes possible through the gift of the Holy Spirit (20:22). John the Baptist designated Jesus as "...the one who baptizes with the Holy Spirit" (1:33); at the Last Supper, Jesus promised to send the Holy Spirit (15:26). That promise Jesus now fulfills for the disciples.

One aspect of this gift of the Spirit is conveyed by Jesus' breathing on the disciples, a gesture that evokes Genesis 2:7, "[T]he LORD God formed man from the dust of the ground, and breathed into his nostrils the breath of life...." (*Spirit, wind, breath* represent the same vocabulary cluster in the Bible.) In the first creation, God's breath brought into existence a human being in the divine image and likeness. Jesus' gift of his own holy wind makes the disciples God's children in the likeness of the Son. Now they are born of Spirit (see John 3:5-6). The breath of God in Genesis gave life. The breath of Jesus in John gives eternal life.

In addition, John relates Jesus' gift of the Spirit to the power to forgive sin: "If you forgive the sins of any, they are forgiven them; if you retain the sins of any, they are retained" (20:23). Jesus was sent as the Lamb of God to take away the sin of the world, according to John; he now shares that power with his disciples. The description of this power as including both forgiveness and binding is related to the fact that the coming of Jesus produces a crisis or judgment. People will opt either for darkness or for light, so that some are condemned and some are not (see John 3:18-21). If Jesus so mirrored God that when people met him they were forced to self-judgment, his disciples must so mirror Jesus that those who encounter them elicit a similar judgment.

### The Reaction of Thomas (John 20:24-29)

In a transitional verse, John tells the reader that Thomas the Twin was absent. The disciples who saw the risen Jesus in 20:19-23 give Thomas the same report that Mary Magdalene had given to them, "We have seen the Lord" (20:25). Because of Mary Magdalene's report, the disciples did not doubt when Jesus appeared to them. But Thomas is adamant in his refusal to believe on the basis of their word. He wants to finger the wounds of Jesus to be sure. Thomas' words reflect an attitude condemned by Jesus in John 4:48, "Unless you see signs and wonders you will not believe." John's Jesus does not reject the possibility that miracles lead people to faith, but he does reject miracles demanded by a disciple as an absolute condition for faith.

That Jesus appears in the same place "a week later" suggests that John's community already held Sunday in reverence as the day of the risen Lord.

Having the time and circumstances of the appearance to the disciples the same as those of the appearance to Thomas is a touch of Gospel irony. Jesus repeats, "Peace be with you," despite Thomas' antecedent doubts! Knowing what Thomas has said, Jesus invites Thomas to examine his hands and side—an invitation that turns the tables on Thomas by probing him. Jesus' words as he challenges Thomas are a query of faith. Thomas accepts the challenge, does not touch Jesus and so professes faith.

The final irony of the Gospel is that the disciple who doubted the most gives expression to the highest evaluation of Jesus uttered in any Gospel, "My Lord and my God!" (20:28). At the beginning of the Gospel, the evangelist told the readers that the Word was God (1:1). Now he has shown how difficult it was for Jesus' followers to come to such an insight.

If the Gospel narrative ended at that point, we would have been satisfied that in John 20 we had seen four different reactions to the risen Jesus. Much to our surprise, the evangelist is interested in a fifth reaction, that of the believer. The final praise for belief in Jesus extends to those who have believed without seeing the burial garments, hearing his voice or recognizing his bodily presence: "Blessed are those who have not seen and yet have come to believe" (20:29). And that, of course, includes all of us.

## Jesus at the Sea of Tiberias and the Miraculous Catch of Fish (John 21:1-8)

The last time in John Jesus was in Galilee at the Sea of Tiberias with his disciples was on the occasion of the multiplication of the loaves (John 6). This chapter implicitly recalls that event. In 6:67-70, Simon Peter took the initiative in speaking for the Twelve: here he again takes the initiative in proposing to go fishing, and arouses the others to go with him. Of the seven disciples listed, one who was mentioned at the beginning of the Gospel reappears here (Nathaniel); four more are members of the Twelve: Simon Peter, Thomas and the sons of Zebedee. It is astonishing that these members of the Twelve who saw the risen Jesus in Jerusalem were sent out by him and given the Holy Spirit as a grant of power over sin, according to John 20, are now simply fishing in Galilee. Thomas in particular has had a special encounter with the risen Jesus, whom he confessed as Lord and God.

But there is no evidence in John 21 that the disciples have been changed dramatically. This chapter effectively warns the readers that a move from belief in the risen Jesus to action based on that belief cannot be taken for granted. The disciples who came to believe in Jesus in John 20 are now engaged in ordinary activity without a sign of transformation. The Gospel writer is about to explain what kind of transformation is required.

The disciples are unsuccessful in their fishing; they catch nothing all night. At dawn Jesus is suddenly present on the shore. Though they have seen the risen Jesus twice before and though Thomas was invited to probe Jesus' hands and side, the disciples do not recognize him. This failure to recognize him, since it shows the limitation of those who have seen the risen Jesus, underlines the beatitude uttered by Jesus to Thomas in 20:29, "Blessed are those who have not seen and yet have come to believe."

Thus far the Gospel of John has presented no scene where Jesus calls men fishing by the lake to discipleship and challenges them to catch people. That scene occurred at the beginning of the Synoptic Gospels as the major initiative of

Jesus' ministry. The Synoptic treatment predicts a future that will come only when the public ministry of Jesus is over.

John offers his miraculous-catch story after the Resurrection with a much more immediate focus. The apostles were sent out by the risen Jesus; yet they have resumed the fishing trade. Jesus now uses that trade to symbolize what they must begin to do. As in Luke, Jesus' assistance reverses human inability to make a catch; so many fish are caught in John 21 that the disciples cannot haul in the net.

The miraculous catch causes recognition of the risen Jesus in a pattern that is somewhat similar to the recognition process in John 20, where we saw a sequence of reactions. The Beloved Disciple believed first, simply on the evidence of the garments in the tomb. Here too the Beloved Disciple is the first to recognize the risen Lord, simply on the evidence of the catch. In John 20, Mary Magdalene was the next person to know him when she heard him call her by name. Here the Beloved Disciple is an intermediary. Simon Peter hears that it is the Lord and immediately jumps into the sea to go to Jesus on the land. The implication is that when one hears the call of Jesus, the response is immediate.

### The Meal of Bread and Fish (John 21:9-14)

Although this episode centers on a meal, what happens is intrinsically linked to the catch of fish and will fill out the missionary symbolism of that catch. In 20:20, the disciples came to experience the reality of the risen Lord only after the Beloved Disciple, Peter and Mary. Here also the disciples, not knowing that it is Jesus, have dragged the net full of fish toward the shore. When they arrive, they see a charcoal fire already burning, with fish and bread on it. Jesus, to them still a stranger, asks for fish from the fresh catch. Simon Peter, knowing that this is the Lord's command, hastens to drag the net ashore. John tells us the net is not broken. What is clear is that the number and the size of the fish show how successful the disciples can be with Jesus' help. This reminds us of 4:37-38, where Jesus sends the disciples to reap an abundant harvest that they did not sow. The symbolism of the unbroken net may be the unity of belief in those "caught" by the disciples in the net of the risen Jesus.

Granted all these reported details of the catch, it is truly astounding that the disciples have not recognized the Lord. John 21:12 at last attributes knowledge to them as Jesus invites them to come and eat breakfast. Other recounted experiences of the risen Jesus are associated with meals: Luke 24:30, 42; perhaps Acts 1:4; 10:41; Mark 16:14. Luke stressed a eucharistic aspect in the meal the risen Jesus shared with the two disciples at Emmaus. John 21:12-13 seems to fit into that situation. Jesus takes bread and gives it to them, similarly the fish, and the disciples know Jesus as the Lord in the context of a meal.

The last time he was at this lake in John's Gospel, Jesus took the loaves, gave thanks and distributed them and the fish (John 6:11). That scene John interprets eucharistically in 6:51b-58: "...[T]he bread that I will give for the life of the world is my flesh.... [U]nless you eat the flesh of the Son of Man and drink his blood, you have no life in you." John wants his readers to reflect on their own eucharistic celebration. As they read how the risen Jesus fed the disciples at the lake, they too are challenged to recognize the risen Lord.

### Jesus and Simon Peter (John 21:15-19)

Several factors in this exchange between Jesus and Peter stand out. Jesus addresses Peter as "Simon, son of John" for the first time since Jesus gave him the name *Cephas* (Peter) in 1:42. In other words, in the Gospel of John this is an address that leads to an identification. The role of shepherd, like the name Peter, signifies this man's special identity in the Christian community.

Before this role is assigned, Jesus asks Peter three times, "Do you love me?" (adding "more than these?" the first time). We are reminded of Simon Peter's boastful reaction at the Last Supper. There, after Jesus warned of the impossibility of following him to the cross, Peter objected, "Lord, why can I not follow you now? I will lay down my life for you" (13:37). Against that background, Peter might well have claimed to love the risen Jesus more than the others, for there is no greater love than the willingness to lay down one's life for one's friend (see 15:13). Moreover, in John 21, Peter hastened to Jesus from the boat while the other disciples did not recognize him and stayed in the boat.

Does Peter still think of himself as the most loving? From his response, apparently Peter has been chastened by his failure in denying Jesus. Jesus does not compare Peter's love with that of the other disciples but asks for a simple, personal affirmation of love. Even in that affirmation, Peter trusts himself to Jesus' knowledge. Previously, when Simon Peter boasted about his willingness to follow Jesus even unto death, Jesus showed that he knew Peter better than Peter knew himself by predicting three denials. Now, although Simon Peter believes with all his heart that he loves Jesus in total fidelity, all that he is willing to claim is "you know that I love you."

There is no doubt, then, that the threefold questioning in 21:15-17 parallels Peter's threefold denial of Jesus in the high priest's court (18:15-18; 25-27). Note that the Synoptic Gospels told us that Peter recalled Jesus' prediction when the cock crowed, but John did not say that. Perhaps we are meant to think that Peter remembers Jesus' prediction only after the Resurrection, reminded by being questioned three times.

Yet the exchange between the risen Jesus and Simon Peter has a more immediate purpose than Peter's repentance. John's Gospel assigns a major pastoral role to him—a highly unexpected role, considering John's theology. The shepherd role that was originally applied to Jesus is now transferred to Peter with the assurance that Simon Peter loves Jesus. The model disciple of this community is one whom Jesus loves. Thus, the mutual love that exists between Jesus and the believers is a most important factor in this community's life. That criterion is applied to anyone who would exercise pastoral care.

**Jesus and the Beloved Disciple (John 21:20-24)**

Despite the exchange just discussed and the unique pastoral role given to Peter, he is not the most important follower of Jesus in the fourth Gospel. The disciple whom Jesus loved was mentioned early in John 21 as the first to recognize Jesus and the one to inform Peter. We now discover that this disciple is still present. It is interesting that this disciple was left without an introduction when first named (21:7), but now John's Gospel introduces him as the one who lay on Jesus' breast at the Last Supper (21:20).

Suddenly this Beloved Disciple is mentioned as following Jesus and Peter, seemingly standing behind them. Is that position a way of hinting that in the estimation of the larger Church Peter the shepherd stands in front? Peter raises the question, "What about him?" Curiously, this disciple, the one whom Jesus loved, to whom no pastoral authority over the flock has been assigned, is a subject of concern to Peter, who has just received authority. Is this because the Beloved Disciple really does not fit easily into a value system established by authority?

In these last verses of the Gospel, we find peculiarly Johannine values exemplified in a striking way. To be a disciple whom Jesus loves is, in the end, more important than being assigned Church authority! If Peter has a primacy of pastoral care, this disciple—the Beloved Disciple—has another primacy bestowed by Jesus' love.


## Conclusion

In sum, the narratives of Jesus' Resurrection in the Gospels are descriptions of the responses of a variety of characters—especially the disciples, both men and women—to God's raising of Jesus. These responses include a variety of emotions and a continued sense of mystery. They leave the modern reader with the faith proclamation that Jesus the Christ rose.

We are called to believe it. How he rose we do not know. We are called to believe that the risen Christ is united with God. How this is so we do not know. We believe that someday we who are followers of Jesus, who believe in him and in the God who works through him, will also rise from the dead. How this will happen to us we do not know.

Ultimately, the Resurrection is apprehended in faith, not in explanation. The Gospels proclaim it; we are challenged to believe it. "Blessed are those who have not seen and yet have come to believe" (John 20:29).

## For Discussion

*1) How do you recognize the risen Christ in your life?*

*2) After reading this chapter, do you consider the Resurrection the most important teaching of Christianity? Why or why not?*

*3) Women play important roles in the Gospel stories of the Resurrection. Does this justify ordaining women?*

*4) Do you sometimes question your faith? How is this similar to or different from Thomas doubting Jesus' Resurrection? What kind of role has questioning played in your religious upbringing?*

## For Further Reading

Brown, Raymond E. *The Virginal Conception and Bodily Resurrection of Jesus.* New York: Paulist Press, 1973.

Fuller, Reginald. *The Formation of the Resurrection Narratives.* Philadelphia: Fortress Press, 1980.

Hendrickx, Herman. *Resurrection Narratives.* London: Geoffrey Chapman, 1984.

Neyrey, Jerome. *The Resurrection Stories.* Wilmington, Del.: Michael Glazier, 1988.

O'Collins, Gerald. *Interpreting the Resurrection.* New York: Paulist Press, 1988.

Perkins, Pheme. *Resurrection: Christian Scriptures' Witness and Contemporary Reflection.* Garden City, N.Y.: Doubleday and Co., 1984.

Perrin, Norman. *The Resurrection According to Matthew, Mark, and Luke*. Philadelphia: Fortress Press, 1977.

Perry, John Michael. *Exploring the Resurrection of Jesus*. Kansas City, Mo.: Sheed and Ward, 1993.

Spong, John Shelby. *Resurrection: Myth or Reality?* San Francisco: Harper, 1994.

Swain, Lionel. *Reading the Easter Gospels*. Collegeville, Minn.: The Liturgical Press, 1993.

CHAPTER NINE

# The Call to Discipleship

If someone asks you, "Why are you a Christian?" your answer may be, "Because I consider myself a disciple of Jesus of Nazareth and a follower of the tradition he initiated."

Discipleship or the following of Christ has been for centuries a way of characterizing the Christian commitment. It is commitment based on allegiance to a Palestinian Jew, Jesus of Nazareth, who more than nineteen centuries ago made an impact on human history that has echoed ever since. Discipleship, of course, can mean many things to many people. Modern Christians need to scrutinize their commitment to Jesus the Christ and assess their degree of involvement.

Part of that scrutiny and assessment has to be measured by the biblical roots of such commitment. Today's Christians are no longer contemporaries of Jesus. His impact on them differs from that made on those who were his privileged contemporaries. What we know of him as an itinerant religious teacher who revitalized a form of Judaism by his "teaching with authority" (Mark 1:27) comes to us on neither videotape nor CD-ROM.

For twenty centuries, Christians have had to depend on the testimony of Jesus' contemporaries who became his followers and propagated his teaching. Allegiance to Jesus today means wrestling with the portraits of him left in the four Gospels. They were drawn and composed more than a generation after Jesus' departure from the primitive nucleus of his followers. As a result, we have four Gospel portraits of Jesus with differing lines, shadows and colors. The Marcan Jesus acts differently from the Lucan Jesus; the Matthean Jesus speaks differently from the Johannine Jesus. Correspondingly, the specifics surrounding the role of discipleship differ in all four Gospels.

The purpose of this chapter is to explore the different understandings of discipleship presented in the Gospels. By the end of this chapter you will have a better understanding of what it means to be a disciple of Jesus, and a new respect for the nuances as the Gospels attempt to wrestle with what it means to follow Jesus.

## Discipleship in the Synoptic Gospels

Matthew, Mark and Luke begin their accounts of Jesus' mission with dramatic calls to discipleship. In Mark 1:16-20 and Matthew 4:18-22, Jesus inaugurates his ministry not with healing or teaching, but by encountering two sets of brothers plying their fishing trade at the Sea of Galilee. Jesus summons the unsuspecting brothers to follow him and to join in his work of fishing for people without preparation or even conversation. Discipleship involves catching people alive for the Reign of God. Simon and Andrew drop their casting nets; James and John leave their father, hired hands and boats. All four immediately begin to follow Jesus.

The Lucan story (5:1-11) is more elaborate, but the same vivid elements are present. In Luke, Jesus has already begun his powerful mission in the Nazareth synagogue (4:16-30) and in the village of Capernaum (4:31-41). Jesus' proclamation of the word now engulfs Peter's partners, James and John. Jesus transforms their frustrating night of empty nets by his potent word. At his command, they come up with a staggering haul of fish. Then, Simon, dumbfounded by Jesus' majesty, is called to catch people. As in Mark and Matthew, these fishermen leave boat and trade and immediately follow their newfound Master.

These eloquent stories of the beginnings of discipleship clearly signal what Christian readers of the Gospels have instinctively recognized for ages: The disciples are mirror images of the Christian. In the hopes and failures of these first followers of Jesus the evangelists sketch the essential qualities and experiences of all followers of the risen Christ.

The dramatic portions of the call stories give us a hint at the major characteristics of Gospel discipleship.

1) The *initiative* in the stories all belongs to Jesus; the disciples are called without preparation or merit.

2) The call is to *follow Jesus*. This vocation is especially clear in the inaugural stories of Mark and Matthew, but appears in Luke, too.

3) Discipleship means *empowerment for mission*. The disciples are not called to learn the art of interpreting the law, as rabbinic disciples were. The Christian disciple is summoned to "catch people," to be involved in Jesus' own decisive mission of salvation.

4) The call demands *response*. The disciples must leave all and set out on the journey of faith.

We can use these four characteristics to reflect on the qualities of Christian discipleship found in the Synoptic Gospels.

**Initiative**

Jesus breaks into the ordinary circumstances of human life and summons a person to begin the journey of discipleship. The Galilean fishermen are merely the first in a string of Gospel characters whose lives Jesus transforms by his magnetic presence. Levi, the tax collector, is called away from his tax booth at Capernaum (Mark 2:13-14). Jesus rescues the man with an unclean spirit from his life among the tombs and sends him out on mission to the Decapolis (Mark 5:1-20). A blind beggar, Bartimaeus of Jericho, has his pleas for mercy and for sight answered, and leaves his pauper's cloak behind to follow Jesus to Jerusalem (Mark 10:46-52). The Twelve are drawn from the inner circle of Jesus' followers and sent out on a mission (Matthew 10:1-8). Jesus liberates women and draws them into his ministry (Luke 8:1-3).

This roster of Gospel characters moves beyond the

explicitly designated disciples in the Synoptics. But the boundaries between "disciple," "apostle" and other followers of Jesus are not clearly explained in the Gospels. All these stories illustrate what the inaugural stories so clearly imply: Christian life is an unmerited gift. Faith is a grace! The Gospels show little interest in the process by which someone might grope their way toward faith. Perhaps this is because the Gospels were written for believers—not as enticement for nonbelievers seeking first conversion, but for Christians hoping to deepen a call they have already received. Therefore, the call is present without ambiguity or preparation to emphasize its essential character as an initiative offered by the Lord.

**Following Jesus**

Men were not the only persons who followed Jesus. This is especially true in Luke's Gospel. If we look at Luke 8:1-3, 23:49, 23:55 and 24:1-11, we notice that Jesus had both named and unnamed female followers. (Luke also mentions women followers of Jesus in Acts 18:1-2.) It would therefore be an improper reading of the Christian Scriptures to hold that Jesus only called *men* to be his disciples.

Practically every page of the Gospels narrates the life of a disciple. The disciples have almost no life of their own apart from their relationship to Jesus. We have brief glimpses of their backgrounds—fishermen, tax collectors, beggars, Zealots—but there is no real biographical interest in the disciples other than their relationship to the Master. The entire focus is on their presence in Jesus' mission of healing and teaching and, eventually, in their reaction to Jesus and his mission.

The disciples are the privileged witnesses to Jesus' awesome Kingdom ministry. As he wades into the pain and confusion of Galilee, the disciples are there to observe the impact. Several times, a few are singled out to be present at such monumental displays of God acting through Jesus as the raising of the daughter of Jairus (Mark 5:21-43) or Jesus' transfiguration on Mount Tabor (Mark 8:2-8; Matthew 17:1-8;

Luke 9:28-36). The disciples alone, bobbing helplessly at sea, witness the great nature miracles of the calming of the storm (Luke 8:22-25) and the walking on the water (Mark 6:45-52). These events eloquently display Jesus' power over chaos, which the ancients often symbolized by water.

Mark's Gospel, in particular, stresses that the disciples are the beneficiaries of Jesus' private instructions. More than once, their Teacher dismisses the crowds to concentrate his explanations on the disciples (4:10; 7:17; 10:23). The disciples, too, are taught to pray by Jesus (Luke 11:1-4). When they are under attack by opponents, Jesus rises to their defense (Matthew 9:14). There is little, if anything of his life that Jesus does not share with the disciples; they are his constant companions.

The Gospels clearly intend to make a statement about our Christian life in portraying this bond between Jesus and the disciples. To be with him and to learn from him is not merely a passing phase in initiation; it is the goal of Christian life. The Gospels ingeniously express this by sketching the life of discipleship as essentially following Jesus. There is no point in the narrative in which the disciples graduate to the status of master. They are always "on the road," following their Lord.

Mark probably deserves the credit for being the first to cast the experience of Christian life into the journey metaphor. The dizzying round of healing and teaching that characterizes Jesus' mission in Galilee in the early chapters of the Gospel gives way to a single-minded journey to Jerusalem. Jesus begins to speak openly of his impending death (Mark 8:31-32). His disciples, hardly comprehending, find themselves drawn into that fateful journey with their Master.

The journey toward Calvary, an eventual victory, dominates the middle part of the narrative in all three Synoptics. Mark 10:32 captures in a single moment the demanding reality of Christian discipleship: Jesus is on the way to Jerusalem, to the complete giving of his life in service, while the dumbfounded and fearful disciples follow along behind him. Matthew adopts the same pattern. Luke seems to develop the journey metaphor even more: in Luke 9:51, Jesus *sets his face* toward Jerusalem and begins the exodus that will carry him to death and final glory. The journey will bring Jesus not only to Jerusalem but also, under the impulse of the Spirit, will thrust the disciples out into the world as witnesses to the risen Christ, a continuing journey of discipleship narrated in Acts of the Apostles.

There is no collegiality in Jesus' Gospel community. The figure of Jesus dominates; he remains elusively out in front, drawing the disciples beyond themselves and their accustomed way of life. Even their relationships with each other are dependent on their relationship with Jesus. When he is arrested and taken away, the bonds break apart in flight and panic. Only when Jesus comes back to the disciples in the triumph of the Resurrection are the bonds renewed and solidified.

There is little need to moralize on these Gospel images. The metaphors of "following" and "journeying with" Jesus have nourished Christian spirituality from the first century to the present day. The images are, of course, subject to much elaboration. Their central statement is clear: Christian life is not an ideology or an ascetical technique or a set of moral instructions. Its essential character is a faith relationship with the person of Jesus Christ; everything else is secondary to and a consequence of that bond.

**Empowerment for Mission**

The Gospels assert without qualification that the presence of Jesus effects transformation. Somehow, to encounter him is to be changed. The tide of broken humanity that flows toward Jesus is made whole: The blind see, the lame walk, those tormented by evil are liberated, the ignorant are instructed, the hungry fed, the dead given life. Some people react with hostility and reject Jesus. But few if any casual observers confront the Jesus of the Gospels and walk away coolly unaffected.

By these stories, the evangelists define the mission of Jesus. For the Synoptics, the dominating metaphor is that of the coming Kingdom (Reign) of God. The person and ministry of Jesus bring to Israel the first taste of God's definitive rule: the longed-for Kingdom that will break the bonds of oppression and pain and realize humanity's dream of freedom and fulfillment.

The Synoptic Gospels present the disciples as having a stake in this mission. Jesus calls the disciples not only to be formed and instructed by him but also to share his mission. The disciples, like Jesus, are to catch people. That intriguing image, fishing for people, seems to echo images in the Hebrew Scriptures: e.g., Jeremiah 16.16. Jesus' mission is captured in the same fierce imagery: Redemption is a labor, a brawling struggle with the power of evil, a mission that is, literally, a matter of life and death for humanity.

The disciples are bonded with Jesus in order to be empowered for this same redemptive mission. In a multitude of ways, the evangelists make this clear. Jesus calls apostles and names them to go on a mission. Their marching orders duplicate the transforming acts of Jesus' own ministry: announcing the Kingdom, healing, casting out evil spirits, teaching (Mark 3:13-19; Matthew 10:11-8; Luke 9:1-6).

The disciples are destined to be the founders of the ideal Israel, the Twelve who will realize Israel's dream of peace and life without tears (Luke 22:28-30). The mission instructions do not minimize the cost of such a mission. Like their mentor, Jesus, the disciples must travel light, expect an atmosphere of hostility and crisis, and be ready to suffer rejection and persecution (Matthew 10:9-42).

Each of the Synoptic evangelists explains the dimensions of the Christian mission. Matthew, for example, emphasizes the universal scope of the mission and the importance of teaching: The risen Jesus sends his reassembled disciples out into the "whole world" to train people in discipleship and to build community (Matthew 28:16-20). Luke's two-volume narrative (the Gospel and Acts) also emphasizes the universal scope of the mission. It is an experience of salvation in word and action rooted in Jesus' journey to Jerusalem. Then, under the impulse of the Spirit, the Good News breaks out of that

Jewish center toward the ends of the earth (Luke 24:44-49). For Luke, the "twelve apostles" play an essential connecting role between the story of Jesus and the story of the Church. They form a nucleus of people who have walked with Jesus from the beginning and will now guide the community as it travels into the far reaches of the Mediterranean.

In all three Synoptics, mission is a constitutive part of the Christian experience. Jesus' followers are to carry out the transforming words and actions of Jesus. That is why the story is told.

**Response**

The inaugural call stories add one other element to the portrayal of Christian discipleship. The invitation to follow Jesus and to share in his mission demands total response. Accounts of those first encounters present that response in ideal terms: Without a moment of hesitation, the Galilean fishermen leave their old life behind and follow Jesus.

Fortunately for the Christian reader, the rest of the Gospel story shatters the idealized picture. Here is a most enticing aspect of the Gospels: The evangelists refuse to idealize the founding members of the Christian community. The disciples are not plaster statues but flesh and blood. The picture, of course, is not entirely negative. The disciples are the inner circle. They are the ones called to be with Jesus and the ones to whom he will entrust his mission. As the Gospel narratives progress, the disciples do participate in Jesus' ministry and come to recognize him as the Christ. But these positive affirmations coexist with stunning glimpses into the disciples' obtuseness and failure. In many ways, Peter epitomizes this.

No evangelist emphasizes this side of the picture more than Mark. The Marcan disciples seem to stumble through the Gospel story. They are baffled by Jesus' parables (Mark 4:13) and perplexed at his teaching (Mark 7:18). Their senses are completely dulled to the meaning of his person and mission (Mark 6:51-52; 8:14-31).

Their failure is not confined to benign ignorance. As the story develops, their lack of comprehension takes an ugly turn. When Jesus begins to speak of the cross, of giving one's life to save it, Peter rudely attempts to stifle him (Mark 8:32). Other disciples argue among themselves about who is the greatest person, or seek after positions of power, while Jesus tries to instruct them on service (9:34; 10:37).

These and many other examples in Mark prepare us for the disciples' stark failure at the climax of Jesus' mission. When the moment of the Passion comes, Judas betrays Jesus, Peter denies him and all the rest flee in panic.

The other evangelists tone down Mark's negative portrayal. Matthew, for example, prefers the label "little faith" where Mark would bluntly say the disciples have "no faith" (compare Matthew 8:26 with Mark 4:40). Because Luke wants to emphasize the crucial role played by the Twelve, the continuity between Jesus and the Church, he soft-pedals their failures in the Passion story. (He does not, for instance, mention their flight at the moment of Jesus' arrest.) Luke notes the efficacy of Jesus' prayer for the perseverance of the Twelve (22:31-32). But neither Matthew nor Luke chooses to omit the chilling fact that Jesus is betrayed by one intimate and denied by another.

Why are these stories of failure included in the Gospels? Here is where the evangelists and their communities dealt with the real cost of discipleship and the process of lifelong conversion. Christian discipleship is not accomplished in the quickly peaking joy of the initial call by the lakeside. Its story winds hesitantly along the road and on the churning sea. Its moments come in glimpses between confusion, bafflement and plain failure. Discipleship is a lifelong process, a change of heart that an infinitely patient Master will effect in spite of our dullness.

From one angle, the wart-laden portraits of the disciples in the Gospels seem crude and unforgiving. But the tone is ultimately one of compassion. In spite of the most abject failure and apostasy, the invitation to reconciliation remains open. Mark ends his story with the discovery of the empty tomb and with the message that Jesus' scattered disciples will see him in Galilee (16:7). Matthew gathers the shattered community on a mountaintop, and the risen Christ sends them into the world as his apostles (28:16-20). Luke's risen Jesus retrieves the disillusioned disciples on the road to Emmaus and sends them back to an ecstatic gathering in Jerusalem where the same reconciling Lord has already left his mark (24:1-35).

The image of the Church that seeps through these narratives on discipleship is not that of a sterile moral elite, but of a fully human community, able to have compassion for weakness without despairing of its call to greatness. The story of the disciples is the Church's story. It is told with disarming simplicity, but carries the power to challenge every believer in every age who has felt the call.

## Discipleship in the Gospel of John

The fourth Gospel is different from the Synoptic Gospels in its approach to discipleship. John presents the call of the first disciples in a series of encounters with Jesus that culminate in Jesus' self-revelatory assertion: "Very truly, I tell you, you will see heaven opened and the angels of God ascending and descending upon the Son of Man" (John 1:51). Three scenes lead up to this climax: the encounter with the first disciples (John 1:35-39), the encounter with Andrew and Simon (John 1:40-42) and the encounter with Philip and Nathaniel (John 1:43-50).

When you compare the fourth Gospel's description of these encounters with those of the Synoptics, you quickly notice that the call of the brothers, Andrew and Simon, has been placed between two longer accounts (John 1:35-39; 43-50), neither of which has any parallel in the Synoptic Gospels. The fourth evangelist seems to focus on the call of Nathaniel, who is not identified by name in any of the other Gospels. Only John describes an initial encounter between Jesus and five disciples. Three of these we know from the Synoptic tradition: Simon, Andrew and Philip. John does not tell us about the call of the sons of Zebedee (Mark 2:13-14).

The fourth Gospel shares with the Synoptic accounts the

call of Andrew and Simon, but it does not offer any indication that these Galileans were fishermen. Unlike Matthew, who capitalizes on Simon's change of name (Matthew 16:17-19), John offers a matter-of-fact description as he recounts his tale of the encounter between Jesus and Simon, son of John (1:42). Strikingly, the fourth evangelist does not even give primacy of place to Jesus' encounter with Peter. Instead he presents Andrew, Simon Peter's brother, as a disciple before Simon is even introduced.

When looking at the fourth Gospel, it is necessary to take these differences into account. A particular focus must be placed on the interplay between Peter and the Beloved Disciple, a tension that heightens the drama of this Gospel.

The Gospel does not mention the Beloved Disciple explicitly in the first chapter. At the outset of his story, the evangelist presents us with the tale of an encounter between Jesus and two disciples. One is later identified as Andrew (2:40), while the other remains anonymous. The evangelist gives his readers a perspective on discipleship before he tells them about any of the disciples, including Peter, whose key role among the disciples had long been told within the Gospel tradition. The story of the first encounter does not appear in the Synoptics because it represents the insights of the fourth evangelist's own community into what it means to be a disciple.

For John, one becomes a follower of Jesus because someone has witnessed to Jesus. John the Baptizer is the witness par excellence when he gives the testimony, "Here is the Lamb of God" (John 1:29, 35) and later when he states that "this is the Son of God" (John 1:34). In John's perspective, discipleship is a consequence of bearing witness to Jesus. By phrasing John the Baptizer's testimony enigmatically, "Look, here is the Lamb of God!" John introduces the reader gently but clearly to symbolism, without which it is impossible to understand this Gospel.

At one level the Gospel is a narrative tale. It tells in a simple way the remembered story of Jesus of Nazareth. The events it recounts are singularly important events in the life of a historical figure who died more than a half century before the Gospel was written.

On another level, the Gospel of John is a symbolic tale. It tells the story of the Johannine community, its faith and its struggles. As the evangelist weaves his account of Jesus of Nazareth, he makes abundant use of symbolic language. His readers are thus able to glimpse his faith convictions and the real-life confrontations those convictions entail.

Having heard the stylized account of John's testimony and having been introduced to Johannine symbolism in the words placed on the lips of the Baptizer, we are prepared to appreciate the tale of the first encounter for what it really is: a symbolic narrative.

> The next day John again was standing with two of his disciples, and as he watched Jesus walk by, he exclaimed, "Look, here is the Lamb of God!" The two disciples heard him say this, and they followed Jesus. When Jesus turned and saw them following, he said to them, "What are you looking for?" They said to him, "Rabbi" (which translated means Teacher), "where are you staying?" He said to them, "Come and see." They came and saw where he was staying, and they remained with him that day. (John 1:35-39)

The symbolism in this story focuses on the use of four verbs that can be understood on the narrative level. The narrative account, however, serves merely as a backdrop for the symbolic account which the evangelist unfolds for his readers. The key words are *follow*, *seek*, *stay* and *see*.

On the narrative level, the story of the encounter between Jesus and the first disciples is the story of two men who had been disciples of John the Baptizer. Intrigued by their hero's testimony about Jesus, they went running after him. Jesus heard their footsteps, turned to them and asked what they were looking for. They addressed him as "rabbi" and asked him where he was staying. Jesus said to them, "come and see." They did and decided to stay.

Rereading the account on the symbolic level, with full attention to the Johannine notions of following, seeking, seeing and staying, we realize that John offers a model of discipleship which we can best appreciate by looking at his dramatic use of language. It invites readers to participate in the unfolding drama. The story of Jesus' encounter with an anonymous disciple is thus a very Johannine tale.

## To Follow

The disciple comes to Jesus because he has been attracted by John the Baptizer's testimony. Immediately he is characterized as a "follower." In the Synoptic tradition, to follow Jesus is to be his disciple. The fourth evangelist shares with the Synoptic authors this metaphorical use of the verb *to follow*. It is prominently featured not only in John's account of the initial encounters between Jesus and his disciples, but also in two strong sayings on discipleship: 8:12 and 12:25-26. The verb also plays an important role in the allegory of the shepherd and the sheep (John 10:4, 14, 27) and the story of Peter's restoration to authentic discipleship (John 21:19-22). By his choice of the verb in 1:43, the evangelist is not so much telling the story of a particular man running after Jesus as explaining the meaning of discipleship.

## To See

According to John's story, Jesus *saw* that the two were following him. The evangelist employs different verbs for "seeing." On the narrative level, *to see* obviously refers to physical sight. Yet, on the symbolic level it suggests full appreciation of reality. Perceiving that they were disciples of John the Baptizer, Jesus invites the pair to deeper intimacy with himself. Although in the Gospel of John discipleship is the result of testimony, it also requires an initiative by Jesus, an invitation to greater intimacy with him.

## To Seek

Jesus directs his concern to the pair with the question, "What do you seek?" These are the first words uttered by Jesus in the fourth Gospel. The *Jerusalem Bible* captures the ordinary narrative meaning of the question by translating the

Greek as "What do you want?"

This opening question introduces us to the search for Jesus, a search that ultimately leads to the cross, where he is found as the revelation of the Father. Jesus' question translated more literally from the Greek might be: "Whom are you seeking?" Disciples are those who search for Jesus.

John's language recalls an ancient Hebrew usage in which the verb *darash* (*zetein* in Greek and *to seek* in English) meant "to interpret [the Scripture]." (*Midrash*, derived from *darash*, means an interpretation of the Scriptures.) In the perspective of the fourth evangelist, Jesus leads us to seek out the meaning of the Scriptures. He not only interprets the Scriptures in an almost academic sense (see John 6:31-33), he is also the one to whom the Scriptures point and in whom they are fulfilled.

The idea that the Scriptures point to Jesus is a leitmotif of the subsequent scene when the disciples exclaim: "We have found the Messiah.... We have found him about whom Moses in the law and also the prophets wrote.... [Y]ou will see heaven opened and the angels of God ascending and descending" (John 1:41, 45, 51). The evangelist anticipates this insight by having the first disciples address Jesus not by his personal name, but as "Rabbi," an interpreter of the Scriptures.

## To Stay

Questioning is an important feature of the fourth Gospel. The evangelist portrays the first disciples as those who question Jesus. Standing on the threshold of full discipleship, yet not fully understanding what it means, they ask: "Where are you staying?" (see 1:38). The *Jerusalem Bible* captures the narrative sense of the disciples' question with, "Where do you live?"

Yet one who is familiar with the Gospel of John as a whole quickly realizes that, from the evangelist's perspective, *to stay* shows not a temporary halt, but a permanent abiding. This full Johannine sense is already familiar to the reader who has twice heard John the Baptizer testify that the Spirit *remains* on

Jesus (see 1:32, 33). On the surface level the disciples' banal question means, "Where do you abide?" On the symbolic and dramatic level of the Gospel, the reader comes to know that Christ remains forever (12:34). The Father dwells in Christ and both of them remain (stay) forever. The disciples and reader are to realize that God and Jesus have pitched their tent in humanity's midst to stay.

**Again, to See**

The appreciation of where Jesus really dwells is, of course, not something to be contemplated from afar. The true disciple is invited to deeper intimacy with Jesus and the Father. This invitation is tendered by Jesus, who says to the exemplary pair, "Come and see." The disciples accept the invitation: "They came and saw where he was staying..." (1:39b). Again, the evangelist has used the verb *to see* not in the sense of physical sight, but of insight—sight accompanied by real understanding.

The acceptance of Jesus' invitation attests that the model pair are indeed true disciples whose following of Jesus has come to fruition. Truly to understand where Jesus abides—in the Father and the Father in him—is to abide with Jesus. Jesus' disciples must abide with him if they are to be fruitful. The disciple is one who abides with Jesus.

From this perspective, the exchange between Jesus and his would-be followers focuses on the invitation to come and see. Those who perceive come to abide with Jesus.

In sum, this is how the author of the fourth Gospel understands discipleship. The disciple is one who has received testimony about Jesus and who enters a dialogue with Jesus. The disciple addresses Jesus with a faith that is superficial but will grow to greater fullness. Finally, a disciple appreciates where Jesus abides and comes to abide with him. Such is John's understanding of the nature of discipleship.

The narrative goes on—and so it must, for the true disciple must in turn give testimony to Jesus. That is how things are on the narrative level, the real day-to-day world in which the disciples of Jesus live. On the symbolic level, where the ultimate meaning of events unfolds, the reader knows that the disciple abides with Jesus. At first the reader of John may be puzzled that the evangelist has left one of the initial pair in anonymity (see John 1:40). The anonymous one is the reader, for the story of the first encounter is the story of anyone who is truly a disciple of Jesus.

## For Discussion

1) *What are the four characteristics of Gospel discipleship? Can you identify them in your own discipleship?*

2) *The Gospels often portray the followers of Jesus as inept bumblers. Do you ever feel the same way about your own approach to discipleship?*

3) *Do you find John's approach to discipleship more mature? Why or why not? In what ways is it different from the approach found in the Synoptic Gospels?*

4) *From your reading of this chapter, how has your personal practice of discipleship been either changed or enhanced? Explain.*

## For Further Reading

Best, Ernest. *Disciples and Discipleship: Studies in the Gospel According to Mark*. Edinburgh: T&T Clark, 1986.

Eigo, Francis A., ed. *A Discipleship of Equals: Towards a Christian Feminist Spirituality*. Villanova, Penn.: Villanova Press, 1989.

Kurtz, William. *Following Jesus: A Disciples' Guide to Luke-Acts*. Ann Arbor, Mich.: Servant, 1984.

O'Grady, John F. *Disciples and Leaders*. Mahwah, N.J.: Paulist Press, 1991.

Stock, Augustine. *Call to Discipleship: A Literary Study of Mark's Gospel*. Wilmington, Del.: Michael Glazier, 1986.

_____. *Our Journey with Jesus: Discipleship According to*

*Luke-Acts*. Collegeville, Minn.: The Liturgical Press, 1990.

Sweetland, Dennis M. *Our Journey with Jesus: Discipleship According to Mark*. Wilmington, Del.: Michael Glazier, 1987.

# Afterword

Jesus is thought by millions to be an important person, by those who call themselves Christian the most important one. In saying anything at all about him, a writer necessarily says too much or too little—possibly both at once.

This book has attempted to encounter the Jesus of the Gospels by looking at different aspects of his origins, life, ministry, teachings, promises and challenges. These are like facets of a precious diamond whose beauty changes at every angle, yet always attracts us by its brilliance.

It is my hope that you have encountered both the beauty and complexity of who Jesus is, how he affects others and how journeying through life with him will cause you to pause in awe at the God you encounter. May you have a newfound respect for the Gospels. May you continue to approach them, invoking the help of the Spirit of God to see what is there. In so doing, may your faith pilgrimage be filled with new insights, adventures and a yearning for what "no eye has seen, nor ear heard" (see 1 Corinthians 2:9b).